Womanpreneur

Womanpreneur

HOW TO CREATE A
6 OR 7 FIGURE BUSINESS
AND
LIVE A LIFE YOU LOVE!

JO DAVISON

A&F
Alice&Fred Books

Alice&Fred Books

First published in Great Britain in 2020 by
Alice & Fred Books
Sidney House
34 Station Road
Tiptree
Essex
CO5 0AZ

ISBN: 978-0-9560965-7-9

Book design and typesetting by Ashdown Creative
www.ashdowncreative.co.uk

DEDICATION

This book is dedicated to:

Team Davison ... Steve, Harry, Louis, Alice-Rose, Emilia and Tilly.

I love my life with you. You are my greatest blessing and happiest achievement. Thank you for choosing me.

AND

You ... the awesome Womanpreneur reading this: You are enough to achieve all your dreams. You deserve it. Keep going.

CONTENTS

‘Whether you think you can or you think you can’t, you’re right’

HENRY FORD

‘All our dreams can come true if we have the courage to pursue them’

WALT DISNEY

INTRODUCTION

Welcome to the world of the womanpreneur. I am very excited you are here.

I'm going to start with a bold statement: This book can transform your business and your life.

Why do I know that? It's because the strategies here have transformed my life, as well as those of hundreds of other women (and men) in business around the world. All of them have set themselves free from all kinds of limiting attitudes that were holding them back in business and life. Now I will show you how you can too.

What is a 'womanpreneur'?

My definition: a woman who owns a business and who wants to have it all! Day-to-day freedom, choice, health, and money to live life and run a successful, profitable, six- or seven-figure business on her terms – and, if she chooses, to be a great mum, wife or partner, and an inspired, confident, happy woman.

Is it possible to achieve this? Unfortunately, many people will tell you it's not possible. I've heard the following comment, or something like it, numerous times over the last few years from fellow women in business:

'Everybody knows you can't have it all! There is no such thing as having freedom, work–life balance, happiness *and* success in business for women.'

I don't agree! I know we *can* have it all *and* we can set ourselves free – if we want it: if we are willing to design our business and our life rather than letting it just happen to us; if we are willing to let go of who we think we 'should' be, how we think we 'should' live and how we feel we 'should' run our businesses. It is perfectly possible to reset our lives so we can be successful on *our* terms.

Womanpreneurs are okay with breaking the rules, living outside the norm, not worrying about what others think. We are busy doing the things others tell us cannot be done!

What do I mean by 'setting yourself free'?

As a fellow womanpreneur, I want you to have it all. I want you to have a successful, profitable six- or seven-figure business on your terms whilst living a life you love. I want you to be happy in all areas of your life. However far-fetched it may sound, I believe the only thing stopping you from 'having it all' and setting yourself free is YOU! The aim of this book is to inspire you to believe you can do just that, and give you some tools to start the process. The strategies I am going to share are exactly what I used to set myself free.

There are two components that must be addressed for a womanpreneur to set herself free:

1. **She needs to unblock herself**. Let go of negative mindset, experiences, and beliefs to free herself to be the person she is meant to be. To be okay with being happy, confident and shining her positive light into the world.

2. **She must create a business model that is empowering.** This way, it allows the womanpreneur to reach all the goals she has for the business – whilst also having time, money, and the choice to not be chained to it. To be free to enjoy both a fulfilled business and personal life.

I used the strategies in this book to create and grow my own seven-figure, dream-lifestyle business that gives me less stress, and more freedom, money and happiness – and, yes, my dream life. To give me freedom on *my* terms. I'm going to show you how you can achieve this too. If I can do it, I know you can!

If you are reading this book you are probably one or more of the following:

- Already a female business owner looking to remove some stress in your business.
- Already a female business owner who is ready to grow your business.
- The female owner of a new start-up business.
- A female thinking about starting a business.

Whatever stage you are at, you have come to the right place. This book is going to help you design a business and life you love, on your terms, and help give you the strategies to set yourself free.

A chance meeting with a blue cow that would change my life forever

A few years back, I still owned my offline health care practices with my husband. I was feeling stressed, burnt out and very frustrated. On the outside we looked successful – our business was busy and we were employing lots of people. But, as the co-owner of this successful business, I was feeling more trapped, more stressed and earning less money than I had done as an employee in someone else's business.

After a period of being terrorised by staff, having money stolen from the till, people going off sick, wearing too many business and life hats (eg. marketing hat, finance hat, HR hat, as well as those for recruitment, business development, customer service, mummy, wife etc.), I was feeling lost, exhausted, fed up with trying to be all things to all people, including a great wife and mummy, and constantly feeling guilty and at the end of my tether. We found ourselves with a staff mutiny on our hands. Everyone was bitching and complaining. They sent us emails listing everything they were unhappy with and all the things we were doing wrong in their eyes. We had been trying hard to create an awesome business yet no one, including ourselves, was happy.

The final straw came when I completely lost the plot one day, and shouted at a difficult client who was complaining. Normally, I would have dealt with this calmly. He was the one being unreasonable but, even so, I was a master at handling difficult customers. That's when I knew I'd reached burnout and that things had to change. They simply couldn't carry on like this; I'd reached my breaking point. We closed the business and told our staff to take a day off. My husband and I needed to regroup, rest and come up with a plan to either change things or close the business forever.

Our day-to-day life had been like a survival challenge, with constant issues, money worries and fear. Don't get me wrong, it was a love-hate relationship: some days I still enjoyed what I was doing. However, it always seemed to be the case that just as something seemed to be going right, the next day we would be thrown another curve ball. Exhausted, we decided to spend some time with our young son, Harry. We asked him what he wanted us to do together that day. It seemed like it had been a long time since we had had a family day that wasn't taken up by business-worry discussions.

Harry wanted us to watch CBeebies (his favourite UK TV channel) and, to be honest, it felt like the last thing I wanted to be doing. However, it was there that we discovered a cartoon. A cartoon that would change my life.

It was about a cow but, unlike all the other cows in her field, she was blue. That was not the only difference: Blue Cow was positive, unique, dynamic and optimistic. She had ideas, and wanted to explore the world outside her field. She didn't want to settle into the life that was expected of 'normal' cows. In the episode we watched, Blue Cow declared that she was going to go to the Olympics because she wanted to compete and feel what it was like to win a gold medal. Rather than encouraging her, the other cows ignored her when she told them her plans. Except for one brown cow, who said, 'She's off again. Everybody knows cows can't go to the Olympics.'

This state of affairs seemed to echo my life so much at that time. Lots of 'well-meaning' people, including staff, friends, family and customers, were frequently telling me 'everybody knows you can't do this or that' when I came up with suggestions for the business's development. I also had these doubtful thoughts in my own head. In the cartoon, Blue Cow had a choice: did she agree, give up on her dream, stay in the field and behave like the other cows, settling for a normal cow life – or did she go and live her dreams? As we watched, Blue Cow went to the edge of her field, crept over the fence, looking scared and excited at the same time, got the bus and went to the Olympics. She left her field! She felt alive, full of possibility, surrounded by positive people who cheered her on. She felt more full of life, more courageous and happier than she had in a long time. On returning to her field, she excitedly tried to tell the brown cows about her adventure. Again, she was greeted with negativity, and most of the cows ignored her. Except for the cow who spoke to her earlier, who said, 'Everybody knows cows can't go to the Olympics.' The narrator replied, 'But, children – we know they can, don't we?'

As the cartoon ended, my husband and I looked at each other across the top of Harry's head. *Woah!* This cartoon was far more profound than, on the surface, it seemed to be. We immediately started discussing Blue Cow and how her approach was applicable to people's lives, including those of business owners. We thought about how Blue Cow business owners would behave if they weren't afraid to create a business of their dreams. We also discussed the attributes and behaviours they would display: bravery, positivity, determination and courage. Then we talked about what it would mean to be a brown cow business owner: settling, wearing all the hats, being negative, grumpy, impatient, remaining frustrated. We created two long lists, one for each. At this moment, I thought that I was probably a Blue Cow – a lost Blue Cow, perhaps, but a Blue Cow nonetheless – who was simply in the wrong field. Then Harry looked up and said, 'Mummy, you're a brown cow.'

I couldn't believe it. Surely Harry meant I was a Blue Cow? Then he qualified his statement: 'You're grumpy like a brown cow.'

In that moment, I had a huge reality check. Not only was the business causing me massive stress, and my staff and customers were unhappy, but I wasn't being a great mum either. Although very upsetting, this was the wake-up call I needed. My husband and I decided, there and then, to change everything: we were going to become Blue Cow business owners who leave their current field and thrive! We would find a way to transform our business and our lives.

We knew it wouldn't be easy. It would test us and our beliefs, and our current way of doing things would have to change. We decided to create a never-been-seen-before, awesome health care business that would reach seven figures without us having to work in it. We would recruit our dream team, set new business and life goals and be determined to change our lives. We wanted to make a positive impact in our community and be fulfilled in our business. So we made the plan and set about achieving it. We got mentors who could help us, studied successful businesses all around the world and took massive action.

After lots of hard work, mindset shifts and strategy change, we turned things around, grew our dream business, attracted our dream team, reached all our goals and financial targets and 'lived happily ever after' (well, mostly). We ended up being approached by other business owners who asked us to show them how to do it, too. But more about that later.

It's never just about the business

Whilst in the process of transforming our business, Harry's comment had stuck with me; in fact, it had really tugged at my heart strings. I wanted to be a great mum *and* have a successful business. I knew that, whilst we needed to change the strategies in the business, I also needed to change *me*. The way I viewed myself, the way I was behaving as a female business owner and leader, had to change. I was being a brown cow. I was working hard, but not smart, trapping myself but blaming others. Much of the time, I was resentful, unhappy, feeling guilty and trying to do too much. I was being led by my fears and limiting beliefs one day, then by the driven entrepreneur inside me the next. It was exhausting, consuming and conflicting.

I was working far too many hours, and allowing myself to try to please everyone else but me. I was also demanding and impatient with my team but blaming my 'high standards'. Yet, at the same time, I loved being in business, trying to run it and grow it. I was just trapped on the rollercoaster I thought was normal for a successful female entrepreneur and business owner. Deep down, I knew that no matter what changes we made in the business, if I didn't work on *me*, ultimately I would still be unhappy.

I had no idea how to change. In fact, I continued in the same cycle until it was really shoved in my face that I needed to change and it had to happen *now*. One day, I went into my business and my then PA informed me that I reminded her of the boss from the movie, *The Devil Wears Prada*. Having never seen it, I took what she said as a compliment. I went home that night and watched it. Oh, my word ...

I was completely gutted. I was working so hard and I really wanted to be a great boss. If you have never seen the film, go watch it and you will see why this comment, in addition to Harry's declaration that I was a brown cow, made me feel like one MASSIVE failure. The boss lady in the movie was a complete bitch.

A Blue Cow Womanpreneur is born

So, I made a list. What behaviours was I displaying at that time that marked me out as a Brown Cow woman compared to those I would display if I was Blue Cow woman? In fact, what behaviours would any womanpreneur display if she was running a successful business and living life on her terms?

Blue Cow behaviour of womanpreneurs

- Confident
- Happy
- Taking responsibility
- Earning the money you want
- Positive self-talk
- Feeling in control
- Taking time off to recharge
- Surrounding yourself with other Blue Cows
- Encouraging others
- Knowing your worth
- Creating business strategies to free you from the day-to-day running
- Being willing to let go of who you've been to become who you want to be
- Being prepared to change the rules for business and life
- Investing in a mentor to help you work smarter, not harder
- Believing in self
- Being a positive leader
- Being okay with saying no to the things you don't want to do

Brown cow behaviour of womanpreneurs

- Negative
- Not confident, putting yourself down
- Stressed
- Frustrated
- Allowing others to put you down
- Being a bad boss
- Being a victim
- Unwilling to change
- Moaning to anyone who will listen about your stress or challenges
- Thinking your past has to be your future
- Staying stuck
- Constantly comparing self to others
- Feeling guilty
- Doing too much
- Not empowering others
- Doing everything yourself
- Never saying no

Reading the list, I was shocked. I realised I was displaying far too much 'brown cow-ness'. I needed to take responsibility for my life and my part of the business and change how I was showing up.

I ask you the same question: who are you being most of the time? Are you expecting a great Blue Cow business yet spending your time acting like a brown cow? Do you want a successful business and happy life on your terms, yet blame others around you for not having that in place? Maybe you are already successful in your business and life, but have been settling, keeping yourself small and in your comfort zone, but knowing that you need to grow? No one is coming to rescue you: you have to create it; yet, you cannot manifest what you do not own.

It begins with us

The most important conversations we have are those we have with ourselves. The voice we hear the most is the voice inside our own heads. If we are constantly listening to a brown cow voice, it's impossible to create a Blue Cow life and business, and we will never become happy womanpreneurs. When I changed how I was showing up, not only did my life and business transform but new opportunities presented themselves, my positive peer group developed, and I was happier and more successful. It will be the same for you and I am excited to show you how.

Free yourself and join the Blue Cow herd

Our Blue Cow strategies have gone on to help thousands of people around the world through our events, our mentoring and our spreading of the Blue Cow manifesto. I knew the Blue Cow *mooo*vement was growing, and that people were transforming their business and their lives, when I was invited to speak at an event in Rome. The day before my talk, I was doing some sightseeing with my husband, and as we walked down a narrow street, heading towards the Colosseum, we heard a shout: 'It's the Blue Cow lady!' I turned around and saw a very well-known speaker from the USA literally running up to us, yelling excitedly.

Here I was, in Italy, being recognised by an idol of mine from the USA, who was shouting about Blue Cow, and I had no idea how he even knew about it. I'd never met him before. As it happened, at that event, instead of mentioning 'Blue Cow' in English, I had to keep saying '*Mucca Blu*'... Blue Cow was going international!

Since then, we have shared the Blue Cow strategies all around the UK, Italy, Spain, New Zealand, the USA, as well as a whole host of places via the online space. I had no idea just how powerful this concept would become. I tell my version of the Blue Cow story and relate it to the life and business strategies we teach. And we have seen massive breakthroughs. We have a global 'mooovement' of Blue Cows who are all striving to 'have it all', creating and running businesses they love and living lives they love too! We also have hundreds of their team members who embrace the Blue Cow ethos. I want this for you too!

I know it may sound crazy, but it doesn't stop there. We hold a Blue Cow Summit and Blue Cow Congress every year, where hundreds of business owners come together to be inspired by Blue Cow thought leaders, who share their life and business insights and expertise. We have a Blue Cow Women in Business retreat, where amazing women come to network, to learn and to grow. I frequently arrive to speak at events, to be greeted by a wave of people dressed as Blue Cows in the audience. *Literally*. Faces painted, wearing Blue Cow ears and onesies. I was once asked to speak on stage dressed in a Blue Cow onesie, which I did, and it went down really well with the audience. It's awesome (and a bit crazy) but that's what Blue Cows do. They're not scared to 'step out of their field' and do things differently, outside of their comfort zone.

I appreciate that the Blue Cow concept is not for everyone. So, if you don't like being called a Blue Cow, then I'm okay with that. Stop reading now, as my mission is to help you unleash your inner Blue Cow and be the successful and happy womanpreneur you were born to be, so you can create a six- or seven-figure business, a life you love, and ultimately set yourself free.

The motivational speaker, Anthony Robbins, says: 'Our life is a direct reflection of the expectations of our peer group'. So for those who resonate with the Blue Cow message, I hope you will join the mooovement. We know that hanging out with fellow Blue Cows helps us to continue to grow and be the best version of ourselves.

Start by joining our free 'Blue Cow Women in Business' Facebook group for some daily inspiration within a like-minded, awesome community:

www.facebook.com/groups/bluecowwomeninbusiness/

My time working on my own businesses, and now with hundreds of mentoring clients and their teams all around the world, has shown me that *every one of us has the choice to live as a blue cow or as a brown cow*. We can choose how we show up and how we respond to what happens to us. Blue Cows get stuff done; they do the things that others say cannot be done; they move towards their goals and dreams. They think BIG! They try to fearlessly see the world in a positive light and make a positive difference. You are a Blue Cow! I know that, or you would have put this book down already! You have stepped up, created or bought a business and are now growing and running it to make your positive difference in the world. The world needs your business product and service! The world also needs an inspired YOU! Others need you to be the beacon of light in the darkness that shows them the way to achieving their dreams by demonstrating how you live yours. So don't dim your light to please people who act like brown cows ...

Marianne Williamson puts it brilliantly:

Our deepest fear is not that we are inadequate.
Our deepest fear is that we are powerful beyond measure.
It is our light, not our darkness
That most frightens us.

We ask ourselves
Who am I to be brilliant, gorgeous, talented, fabulous?
Actually, who are you not to be?
You are a child of God.

Your playing small
Does not serve the world.
There's nothing enlightened about shrinking
So that other people won't feel insecure around you.

We are all meant to shine,
As children do.
We were born to make manifest
The glory of God that is within us.

It's not just in some of us;
It's in everyone.

And as we let our own light shine,
We unconsciously give other people permission to do the same.
As we're liberated from our own fear,
Our presence automatically liberates others.

So let's stop settling, the self-doubt, the 'not earning as much money as we deserve', the stress and fear – let go of our 'brown-cow-ness' and get to work!

Why a book for women in business?

I didn't set out to be a business mentor, consultant, speaker and author or to specifically work with women. A few years ago, my husband and I became well known in the health care business niche. Our health care practices were growing and thriving and, as a result, other practice owners would approach us and ask for help with making their practices more successful. We started helping them for no charge and actually began spending more time in their practices than we did in our own business. On one level this was fine because we had created a seven-figure business that would run without us being there if we didn't want to be. This allowed us to run a business that we loved, surrounded by our dream team, whilst also having more time, more freedom and less stress. However, a pivotal moment came when a fellow business owner took me out for coffee and, after two hours of 'picking my brains' said, 'That was great. So much more useful than the sessions with my business coach that I'm paying for.'

I paused and asked, 'What's a business coach?' He told me how a guy came in and helped him with his business.

So I went home and said to my husband, 'Do you realise people get paid for doing what we're doing for free and what we love to do?'

As we had a passion for sharing our business success strategies, he said we should investigate.

The second 'nudge' came when a flyer popped through our door advertising someone else's business mentoring services. On it was a testimonial from someone I'd worked with for free over coffee – someone I knew had been helped by our strategies even more than they had by this business coach they were promoting, because they'd told me. Although I didn't have any official coaching qualifications, I had business experience: I'd started a business from scratch, grown it to seven figures, and employed team members. Not only that, but, by now, I'd been working (for free!) with lots of business owners and had realised that many of the same business and life challenges came up for them, too, and our strategies were transforming those business owners' lives.

So, we launched our business mentoring company.

It's different for women

After a couple of years, I started to see a pattern. Our female clients were often dealing with additional challenges that weren't shared by their male counterparts: trying to run their businesses while attempting to have a balanced life and feel free. I'm not saying it's harder for women, simply that some of their challenges are different. Despite my female clients working in disparate businesses, some big, some small, in different countries and industries – the same challenges presented themselves time and time again. And I could relate, as I'd experienced many of them too.

Some of the main challenges are: how do you balance growing and running a successful six- or seven-figure business with being a wife, MD of your home, mummy, friend, relative *and* stay happy, healthy and balanced? How do you stop feeling the constant pressure of trying to do it all, and never quite getting there? How do you stop the worries about money? How do you overcome the challenge of not having enough time? How do you stop the voice in your head that tells you regularly that you are not good enough? How do you deal with the guilt that often comes when you think you should be at home with the kids when you are at work, and at work when you are home with the kids? How do you manage to get to the gym, maintaining a positive healthy relationship with yourself, as well as giving time to your significant other and friends? I hear these challenges from women in business (before they work with me) every day!

I run a successful international business, with mentoring and consultancy clients in multiple countries, different time zones and languages. This takes some managing. However, I am also mum to four kids, which, if I am honest, sometimes takes just as much (if not more) managing! Although my husband is awesome and a great dad, I'm the one primarily in charge of childcare and our home. I know many womenpreneurs where this is the same. In order to stay sane (I know that sounds a bit extreme but I think it's a fair evaluation of the situation), I've had to attempt to master the balancing of all areas of my life. It's not easy. I know what it's like to feel overwhelmed and stressed-out one minute, motivated again the next. As I said, it is not easy, but I have created a system that means I can do both in a way that makes me feel successful and free. Freedom is high on my list of values. Why have a business if it does not give you freedom? This is why I love to help other womanpreneurs 'have it all' and gain their freedom in their business and life. Every womanpreneur deserves to run a business they love, earn lots of money, and have fun doing it, whilst living a happy home life, with or without kids.

A couple of years ago, I received this private Facebook message from a stranger:

'Hi Jo, this is all going to sound totally mad. I've just seen that you posted in the xxx group about a housekeeper. Unfortunately, I'm not applying. I have my own chaotic house I struggle to keep in order already. Now this is not something I've ever done before, messaging a total stranger, but I clicked on your profile purely through jealousy that you can afford a housekeeper and I can't, and all I could see was a woman who looks like a fantastic role model and is proving just how amazing women can be! You look like the woman I want to be. I want to be where you are but I'm now terrified that with two kids I'll never be able to achieve it. How did you get where you are? Did having kids not stop you? I don't know why but I feel like you're the woman that can help me ... totally crazy I know! Sorry lol.'

I felt honoured that this fabulous lady had reached out to me, and that's one of the things that actually gave me the gentle nudge to write this book especially for womenpreneurs. I had been thinking about it for a while, and then other things would come up. However, I knew with my strategies, this lady could achieve a successful business *and* be an awesome mum to her two kids – *if* she chose to do so.

This book isn't where I'm going to tell you how perfect I am and how you need to be perfect too. Perfection is overrated! This book is going to share my insights and the strategies I've used to create multiple six- and seven-figure businesses of my own, while still being successful on *my* terms, enabling me to be a busy mum, wife, MD of my home, staying (relatively) sane and actually liking myself in the process. What excited me the most, even more than the success I have achieved for myself, is how much I love giving these same strategies to my fellow womanpreneurs, and I am so thrilled to know that they have now helped hundreds of others achieve their definition of success and freedom too.

So what is my 'secret formula' to having it all and setting yourself free?

I call this process The R.E.S.E.T Formula. There are five steps that must be followed and implemented for transformation to occur.

R: Review
E: Emotional freedom
S: Self care
E: Empowering business model
T: Take action

If you implement these steps, your business and life will never be the same again.

Now is your time to have it all! To set yourself free. It's your time to shine! So let's unleash the even more magnificent and successful womanpreneur inside you.

Much love,

Jo

PART ONE

It's all about you

1
REVIEW

'When writing the story of your life, don't let anyone else hold the pen.'

HARLEY DAVIDSON

The R.E.S.E.T Formula starts with 'Review'. If we don't know where we have been and where we are right now, we cannot know where we are going.

Have you ever faced these challenges?

Wanting to:

- Grow your business
- Feel more successful
- Have financial freedom
- Balance running a business, leading a team, being a mum and wife, ensuring your home is well organised and there's food in the fridge
- Have more kids but not sure if you can handle it or you're not able to get pregnant
- Have a six- or seven-figure business and lots of money in the bank

You're constantly:

- Spinning all the plates
- Rushing around with a never-ending 'to do' list
- Comparing yourself to other women in business, thinking you should be further along and have achieved more
- Comparing yourself to other mums and feeling inadequate
- Feeling you're not reaching your financial goals quickly enough
- Getting stressed about business
- Not sleeping
- Feeling terrorised by negative staff
- Lacking confidence
- Feeling guilty when at work, feeling guilty when at home
- Feeling guilty generally
- Worrying about money
- Worrying about getting new clients or customers
- Knowing you're successful but feeling 'this can't be it'
- Feeling anxious

- Being grumpy and feeling tired but still having to keep going with tasks
- Not having enough time to achieve everything you want to get done
- Feeling plain worn out
- Not feeling enough

I've faced all this too!

How did we find ourselves here?

So, I'm going to 'pee off' a few of you now. Anyone who loves to bitch, moan and blame others, yes, you may get annoyed. But the truth is, we find ourselves here because we put ourselves in this position. We allow it – even if we don't like to admit it. Being a womanpreneur is a choice, and how we choose to live – our success, our stress and our freedom – is our decision. If you are currently not where you want to be, maybe you are hearing a brown cow negative voice in your head right now, saying, 'No, It's not my fault'. Please stay with me for a bit longer. Be open minded and trust me when I say: it is our own fault *and* it doesn't have to be this way. We cannot control what has happened to us in the past. However, we can control how we respond to what has happened in the past, *and* our past does not have to be our future.

If someone advertised the following job, we all know, deep down, that only a *crazy* lady would apply:

POSITION AVAILABLE:

Wonder Woman

Full-time business owner/wife/partner/mother and managing director of home.

- 20 hours per day
- Tasks include: EVERYTHING that needs to be done (sometimes including the work you are paying others to do)

JOB DESCRIPTION:

Full-time business owner

- *Getting new clients*
- *Working with clients*
- *Making sales*
- *Recruiting team members*
- *Leading team members*
- *Marketing*
- *Sales – meeting sales targets*
- *Customer care – ensuring your customers are well looked after*
- *Making products or delivering the service*
- *Finance manager – wealth creation, paying bills, balancing accounts*
- *Social media management*
- *IT – all things technical*
- *Putting out fires/dealing with issues*
- *Stationery and stock ordering*
- *Cleaning*

Full-time mum

- *Growing and delivering a baby (or adopting one), then looking after it so it's safe, fed and watered*
- *Getting kid(s) to school before the bell rings – in correct outfits, with snacks, drinks and school bags*
- *Volunteering on school trips, running stands for PTA events, baking cakes for the cake sale*
- *Organising birthday parties, attending birthday parties with a gift, remembering jeans for jeans day, creating a nativity play costume from scratch*
- *Having play dates frequently so your kids don't feel left out*
- *Remembering when swimming kit/PE kit are needed for school*
- *Being a taxi service*
- *Being a bank and providing the cash*

Full-time wife/partner

- *Being sexy, bold, feminine and looking 'hot' at all times*
- *Being energised enough to want to have passionate 'lovin' regularly*
- *Being supportive and encouraging*
- *Being a good listener*

Managing Director of your home

- *Ensuring it runs like a well-oiled machine; contains food; clean, ironed clothing; is tidy, free from dust and ordered at all times*
- *Ensuring meals are cooked*
- *Ensuring holidays are organised, booked and packed for*
- *Ensuring the dog is fed and walked – every day*
- *Ensuring piles of washing are not left on stairs/tables and are put away in the right place*

TERMS:

- *You will be constantly trying to please (delete as appropriate): kids, husband/wife, partner, clients, staff, friends, family, pets and never feeling quite enough*
- *You will be rushing around most days multitasking*
- *Pay: to be confirmed (but it won't be anywhere near what you deserve)*
- *Holidays: you can have them but will spend them busily rushing about and will need a holiday after you return from a holiday*

If you are the right candidate for us you will:

- *Have unlimited energy and be prepared to get worn out*
- *Put everyone else above yourself*
- *Be highly ambitious*
- *Be slightly mad*
- *Be happy to do unpaid overtime*
- *Be a people-pleaser*
- *Possibly be someone who's at risk of letting others walk all over them*

- *Be someone who can live a rollercoaster of highs and lows and exist just on the edge of sanity...*
- *Not be willing to take ownership of your life and change it*

Logic tells us that reading this advert for these four full-time positions, which we would have to carry out AT THE SAME TIME, we would all run away, screaming: 'That role is not for me!' Unfortunately, many of us have not done that. We have unwittingly created and accepted this very situation, meaning we are juggling loads of balls and wearing far too many hats. BIG TIME. Every single day.

It's our fault!

Unfortunately, the truth is, we only have ourselves to blame. Many of us are on the go from the break of day until after dark in the pursuit of balancing our businesses and family lives. We treat our mobile phones better than we treat ourselves – at least we put them down to charge and give them a rest at the end of every day! Many of us allow ourselves to feel guilty if we rest, take a day off, delegate, allow our family to help out, show vulnerability or ask for help. We get irritated by well-meaning loved ones who say, 'You should slow down', 'You're doing too much' or 'You should take a break'. After all, how on earth do they know what we're going through and how much we have to do? We keep saying yes to other people's requests and adding to our never-ending 'to do list'. *And*, because we are ambitious, we strive to achieve more and more of our business and life goals. Our working hours often get out of control.

What we fail to realise is that this is us exhibiting negative womanpreneur brown cow behaviour. For some, I could even go so far as to say our egos are out of control. This was me in the past. When I knew I had to change, I remember thinking, I can do 'stressed out, over achieving, busy businesswoman *and* rushing around mummy' really well. Who would I be if I changed this and became an unstressed, goal smasher and calm mummy? I don't know how to be that person.'

If we don't change, things don't change. We stay trapped in the 'I have to be stressed, unhappy, work long hours, trade my time for money and do everything myself' illusion.

For example, have you ever thought any of the following?:

- I am the only one who can do this admin task well enough. (Nope, you need to learn to delegate better)
- If I don't do it myself, it won't get done. (Nope, you need to get a better power team)
- I can't take a break as I have so much to do. (If you don't take a break, you become exhausted and potentially a moaning brown cow pain in the arse)
- I am very important and have to be there in my business at all times. (Yes, you are important. However, let's keep things in perspective here. Your business will still be there if you take the day off, especially if you design it that way)
- If I say 'no', I am a bad person. (If you can't say no, you spend your life pleasing everyone but yourself. You *cannot* achieve your goals and dreams this way)
- Self-care is luxury. I don't have time to exercise and take care of my health. (Nope, it's just a matter of time before your body or mind will *make* you take a break, normally with an awful health scare or worse)
- If I ask for help, I am weak and unsuccessful. (Trying to do everything yourself makes you a negative womanpreneur brown cow! You are not empowering yourself or anyone else)
- If I admit I want to have more time with my family, partner or kids I won't be seen as successful. (NOOOOO! One of the reasons we have a business is to design a life we love! A successful business will give you *more* time, *more* freedom and *more* choice)

- I have no choice. Being mummy has to come second to my business if I want a successful business. (NOOOOOOOOO! This is a complete illusion and lie. You *can* be a happy, successful mummy *and* own a successful business)
- I have to work the nine to five, *and* extra on my business. (Nope, you can *completely* re-invent your working hours and how you work, if you want it enough)
- Only single women can have a successful business. (NOOOOOOOOOOO!)
- Only a woman who has a man can have a successful business. (I am not even going to comment on that one!)

I can relate to many of these comments, as I've been there ... but business and life do not have to be this way. You can completely change it all. However, you will have to be prepared to *think* differently, *do things* differently and perhaps even *let go* of who you are being right now.

Where are you right now?

Imagine you are sailing on a boat on the ocean. Ahead of you are lots of islands. One of them is your *ideal* island but, unfortunately, you don't know which one it is. So, as you sail, you arrive on one – any one – without realising this is not your ideal island. So, you set up your life here. While you're there, living on the wrong island, you may complain and moan and start to settle. But, the thing is, even though you're on the wrong island, it's not all bad. There are some bits that are actually okay – great, in fact. Yet you still live in a way that is seeing you settle, whether that's with regard to yourself and your goals, your relationships, or your finances. You get confused, and forget what it is you want in business and life. Even if you do know what else you want, it's scary to decide to make the change in order to create a life you love. Just as Blue Cow experienced in the cartoon, deciding to leave our island and make changes is frightening for us.

Sadly, this is how many people live their whole life, instead of designing their island (life) so they know exactly where they are heading and are giving themselves the best opportunity to live happily. They find themselves living a life that just happens *to* them, often giving power away to others. They lose their 'why' and become womanpreneurs who are lost. Being 'lost' can make us fearful, stressed, stuck, frustrated and unwell.

IT IS TIME TO STOP THIS NOW, TO EMPOWER YOURSELF AND TAKE BACK CONTROL OF HOW YOU LIVE YOUR LIFE.

What is your ideal island? And what does 'having it all' and being free mean to you?

I want you to have it all! I want you to set yourself free. Whatever that means to you. Our dream business and dream life is not the same as other people's. A powerful exercise I do with my clients is to help them design their 'island' (dream life). They have to literally draw an island as a representation of their life, listing all the things they want to experience in their life and business. We look at a variety of areas, including:

- Business
- Wealth
- Health
- Self-care
- Relationships
- Family
- Money
- Time
- Holidays
- Hobbies
- Contribution
- Legacy

Then, using the steps in this book (and often with some firm 'supportive' mentoring), we go and create it.

Womanpreneur action step

Get a blank sheet of paper and a load of colouring pens. Draw the outline of a large island on the paper. Divide the island in half. On the left, write down all the things you DO NOT WANT in your life anymore. Don't over-analyse, just believe things can change. On the right, write down all the things YOU DO WANT in your life moving forward. Consider what you love now, and then add in what you want in the future, material and non-material.

If we don't know where we are going, we'll end up somewhere but it won't be on our dream island. We certainly won't end up 'having it all' or 'being free' on our terms. The island you design will be the basis of the decisions you make, the actions you take *and*, therefore, the OUTCOME you achieve for your life. You will need to regularly ask yourself: 'Is what I am doing right now taking me towards my dream island?'

Don't worry at this point if your negative womanpreneur brown cow voice starts telling you:

- I can't do this
- I can't afford this
- I don't deserve this
- I won't be able to do or to have that
- I don't know what I want
- What will people think?
- I'm not good enough, etc ...

I started with those limiting beliefs too! Stop keeping yourself small, it's time to dream BIG. So just create your dream island on paper

– as if money, time, childcare, qualifications, relationships and confidence are not a challenge. And trust me!

I know it's maybe hard right now to decide upon your dream island, but you must. The other day I was driving my older children to school and asked them the simple question: 'What do you want for tea?' The responses varied from, 'dunno' to 'whatever'. I said to them, 'You must decide what you want or you will get dinner but it won't necessarily be the dinner you wanted.' It's the same for us womanpreneurs: we need to stop allowing things to just happen to us or settling with 'whatever' – and *decide* exactly what we want in all aspects of our life. Then ensure we get it.

Consider these two *very* important questions:

1. WHAT BUSINESS DO YOU WANT?

2. WHAT LIFE DO YOU WANT?

When I ask my consulting clients, many will tell me everything they *don't* want, but cannot tell me what they *do* want. It is a common challenge, often due to either the womanpreneur having lost her way, got stuck and is settling, or settling because she does not know what else is on offer or she doesn't believe she can achieve it.

Decisions, decisions: your bigger island picture

So, with this in mind, let's drill a little deeper.

1. What does 'having it all' and 'setting yourself free' mean to you?
2. What things would need to be in place within the next 24 months for you to have it all and set yourself free (on your terms)?
3. What things would you no longer have in your life?
4. What would you need to change to feel like you had it all?

5. List 20 things you would like to experience in your lifetime (or in the next 10 years).
6. Which of these can you/are you going to make happen in the next 12 months?
7. How much money would you like to earn a month?
8. How much money would you like to earn a year?
9. How would your life change if money was abundant and you never had to worry about having enough?
10. What things would you do with your newfound wealth?
11. If you had more time, what would you do with it?
12. What things and experiences would you make happen if time and money were no problem?

Taking back control by clarifying your values

To have it all, set yourself free, and create the life you love, your values are your foundation. Are you living a life in which your daily words and actions match your values? Ask yourself what values are important to you. Here are some examples. **Circle your top 10 or add your own to this list:**

abundance adventure art authenticity
balance beauty
calmness charity community compassion courage creativity
empathy equality excellence excitement
family fitness friendship freedom of choice fun
generosity global peace
harmony health humour
independence inspiring others integrity intelligence
joy

kindness knowledge
laughter leadership living your dreams love for yourself
love for others
music nature passion personal growth pleasure
positive attitude
quality of life reliability
sensuality spirituality
taking risks tidiness time freedom trust
wonder and awe

Write down five occasions when you truly felt yourself. What values were you expressing?

Your life purpose

What is the purpose of your life? Do you live in line with your personal values, desires and dreams? Your purpose is the essence you contribute to the world simply by being the unique human being that you are, rather than because of what you know, own or can do. Knowing your purpose gives you a sense of significance and will propel you to create a life that you love and deserve. To live your life to the full, to have it all on your terms, you must know what you want to do, you must enjoy doing it and you must believe in what you are doing.

1. Write down five things you are most passionate about.
2. Make a list of 10 of your unique skills and abilities.
3. If you had a magic wand and you could wake up tomorrow, doing your dream work, what would that be?
4. Imagine it's your 100th birthday party celebration. What five key achievements would you want to be celebrating as you look back at your life?

5. Clearly define what success in life looks like to you – both in terms of day-to-day and overall.
6. What legacy do you want to leave behind?

Your ideal day

We only live once, so we deserve to spend our days doing what we love. I don't mean when we retire, I mean throughout our lives. What is your ideal day? Spend some time considering this. Think about the following questions:

1. Where do you wake up?
2. Are you alone? If not, who is with you?
3. When you get out of bed and put your feet on the floor, what do you feel? Carpet, floorboards?
4. When you head into the shower, is it an ensuite? What is it like?
5. What kind of soap do you use? What are your towels like?
6. Where do you get dressed?
7. What clothes do you put on?
8. Where do you eat breakfast? Who with? What food do you have?
9. How are you going to spend your day?

Consider every aspect of it, listening to your Blue Cow womanpreneur voice of abundance, where anything is possible.

Create your dream board

Design a life you love. Take a morning to create your dream board. Consider every area of your life and cut out pictures and words that represent it. Stick them on some card and put it somewhere you can see it every day. These are some of the areas to consider:

- Business
- Wealth
- Health
- Investments and savings
- Relationships
- Hobbies
- Fun
- Contribution

Then place it somewhere so that you can see it every day. Ask yourself, are you creating this life right now? If you do not take action, and just stare at the board, don't be surprised if things don't change. You, of course, need to take action to manifest what is on the board. I only do my board for the year ahead. Others make infinite boards. Do whatever suits you, but push yourself. Put on some things that you want to be, do or have, but as yet have *no idea* how you will make them happen. Make at least one thing scary. You never know, it may just come true!

Womanpreneur

'Reset Moment'

- Start to believe that, as a womanpreneur, you are a Blue Cow, who can have it all
- Know that if you settle in your life, you will end up pleasing everyone but yourself
- No one is coming to rescue you, and you don't need them to. You have everything within you right now to create a business and life you love
- Empower yourself and decide to take back control TODAY
- Your past does not have to be your future

2
EMOTIONAL FREEDOM

'Mastering yourself is true power.'

LAO TZU

So the first step in setting yourself free, achieving your six- or seven-figure business and creating a life you love is to REVIEW and DECIDE exactly what you want! The second step requires us to free ourselves emotionally from past experiences, mindsets and beliefs that hold us back from achieving this. Many of the challenges listed at the start of chapter one – for example, feeling guilty, not feeling good enough, rushing around trying to please everyone else, worrying about your business – are mindset and belief challenges that influence our behaviour. Some of these beliefs were created long ago and, without us realising it, they are holding us back.

Were you 'trained' to be a good girl?

'Be a good girl.' How many times do we get told that as a kid? I know that I was a fully subscribed 'good girl' from an early age. Being a good girl had rewards at the time: I didn't get in trouble and I got lots of praise from those around me. I felt loved as a good girl and worried about not being loved if I was not a good girl. Being good meant that I was conforming most of the time: always being agreeable, never being difficult or making a fuss. I always wanted to make everyone around me happy and sought their approval. Doing what I wanted, especially if it upset others, was not allowed (in my view). So I conformed. I sought approval and gained it by being 'good'.

Good manners.

Good behaviour.

Doing as I was told.

Fitting in nicely.

These are not all bad traits to have. However, good girls are sometimes *not* very good at:

- Coping if they upset others (even if it was not on purpose)
- Saying no
- Standing up for themselves
- Standing out
- Making decisions that other people may not like
- Not caring about being seen as selfish (this is different to actually being selfish)
- Asking for help
- Being vulnerable
- These traits will affect our business success and happiness in life.

Now, it goes without saying that having manners and being polite and considerate are very important in society – and for us as business owners and leaders – and, of course, being a team player is vital in business. However, not at the detriment of our own happiness. Not if we're unable to make decisions confidently – ones which serve us and allow us to lead in an empowered way. Not if it results in us becoming lost, frustrated, stressed, depressed and unhappy. Not if we feel the need to work far too many hours and become obsessive. There is nothing to feel guilty about in taking control of our lives and making decisions that lead us towards joy and happiness. Our being happy doesn't mean that someone else has to be unhappy. There is enough happiness to go around. Plus happiness is infectious, if you are feeling happy it may well impact those around you in a positive way. Win win.

As a womanpreneur, you have to be okay with *not* always being a 'good girl' in the way you may have been 'trained'. Staying in this role will often lead us to burnout, frustration, ill health and unhappiness. You are not an employee in your business. I know this sounds obvious. However, the reason I say it is because I hear 'good girl' womanpreneurs telling me frequently that they feel guilty if they're not in their business constantly, especially if they are paying team members to be there. They worry things will fall apart if they take time off. They may worry about what the team or customers will think of them if they do not work long hours. They never say no. They feel bad if they pay themselves well, or spend money on themselves, take nice holidays, drive awesome cars or create a life that gives them freedom. If they do manage to create more time and money, they worry others may disapprove. So they settle. Many start to think small.

This question was recently posted in my private coaching forum:

'I have a question for those of you who are 'out' of your businesses but still own them ... How did you justify it to yourself and also your team? I am increasingly looking to be coming away from seeing clients, and my reasons are this:

Spending more quality time with kids, especially as eldest starts school and I would hope to be able to drop him and pick him up every day (at the moment, I would only be able to do that 3/5 days for both pick-up and drop-off).

My own mental and physical health which are both much better since starting Blue Cow and Jo's coaching but I need to dedicate more time to both!.

Time to pursue the bigger goals of specialising further in my areas of interest.

My limiting beliefs are that my team will just think I'm being lazy/ suiting myself instead of mucking in like the rest of the team. As an example, if one of my team wanted to come in late on all of their morning shifts to drop their kid off at school it would have to be a no! So how can I justify it?'

This was written by an awesomely inspiring womanpreneur. The 'good girl' part of her was in conflict with the business owner part of her. I have seen this *hundreds* of times when clients start working with me, and felt it myself in the early days of my business.

So what is the answer?

We need to change our 'good girl' beliefs and realise that we *can* be, do and have ANYTHING we want. If we allow ourselves. It does not make us a bad girl or a nasty, mean person. As the owner of the business, your role is different from the team you employ. The team is there to do the job you employ them for. If you employ practitioners, they are there to see the patients. If you employ beauty therapists, they are there to see clients. If you employ people to iron, they are paid to iron. If you employ a receptionist, they are there to run reception. This is completely separate from what *you* are there to do.

Now, some people are owner operators, meaning they do carry out part of the same role as their team, which is fine. However (and it's a *big* however), your main role *must* be to use your expertise to grow and lead the business. You cannot do the same role and hours as your team *and* run the business. You will find yourself wearing too many hats. Your priority is to be the leader, so that you provide secure employment for your team and lead them in the most inspiring way you can.

Womanpreneurs must have a different role to their employees: if you lead with your 'good girl mindset and behaviours', the business will struggle – and so will you.

Let's look at the tasks that only a womanpreneur can do and that your employees generally don't:

- Set the intention and vision for the direction of the business as it grows
- Make decisions that not everyone will like, but that will take the business in the direction you want it to go
- Oversee the leadership of the business

- Carry out the 'expert' tasks
- Ensure that your business is meeting its targets and growth so that all the employees have secure employment
- Ensure the financial success, and that everyone and everything gets paid on time

If the good girl part of you is leading, you may find yourself:

- Overworked
- Serving everyone but yourself
- Paying everyone, and not yourself
- Doing the jobs you are paying others to do
- Listening to others who are thinking of themselves (and *not* the business, team, or you)
- Find yourself getting bullied, or making decisions just for an easy life

I used to have the same fears and worries as my client. However, once I realised I had to let go of the good girl, I had to completely change my mindset from being the 'same as everyone else' (who I was employing) to being the visionary and leader of the business. We owned a health care business, so I had been seeing patients. As I started to step back from seeing patients, although our business was growing, it brought up lots of different emotions and thoughts:

- What would my patients think if I wasn't there for them? Would it make me a bad person?
- Some of those patients had been with me for years. Was I being unfair?
- What would my team think if I started to choose my own hours and came and went when I wanted? Would they think me lazy, or be resentful?

1. My husband really helped me with this by reminding me that my patients would be very well looked after by my team. I wasn't leaving, I was simply changing my role. So they would still be able to connect with me but someone else would be giving their clinical care. I would still oversee their clinical care, and see them at times, too, when I was in the centre and they happened to be there.
2. On the whole, my team didn't actually care. They knew how hard I worked and not one of them ever raised the concern that they felt I was a slacker. If they had, it would have been unfounded as I am one of the hardest-working people I know. (And I bet you are too!)

Going back to the post on my private coaching forum and the comment, 'If one of my team wanted to come in late on all of their morning shifts to drop their kid off at school it would have to be a no!' You will recognise it as an example of the 'good girl' not wanting to be seen as mean or unfair. However it is not mean or unfair. Your employees are not the business owner, so of course it would be a no. If the employee wants to come in later after the school run, but his working hours need him to be at work, then he should consider leaving, if he doesn't like working those hours, and take the risk and responsibility of running a business himself! As an employee, he has no risk, no responsibility, no ownership. He can walk away any time he chooses. And when he goes home at night, he is not thinking about the business, the bills or the team, as the owner will be. If the 'good girl' womanpreneur says yes to every team member working only the hours they want, because they feel guilty (unless they have a virtual business with a virtual team where this is by design), the business will fail. You are not a bad girl if you say no to ridiculous employee requests. Interestingly enough, most times I have found that the employees have not even made the ridiculous request – the womanpreneur has invented the worries in her head!

Another client of mine and I were discussing their business opening hours and it became clear that this business was losing a potential opportunity to earn money as it wasn't open on a Saturday. Saturdays would be a prime opening time in their niche. When I asked the business owner why they were closed on that day, the answer was, 'Because I don't want to ask my team to do anything I'm not prepared to do myself, and I don't want to work on a Saturday.'

I hear this a lot. However, this is not an entrepreneurial, womanpreneur mindset, it's an employee mindset. The hours we choose to work and the hours our business is open to serve customers are two very separate things if we employ a team. Of course, it's different if your business is you providing a service on your own. Then you should set the hours that you want to work.

I explained to the owner that they should consider reviewing their mindset about this. The business not being open on a Saturday was not a good business decision in their case. If they did open it, that wouldn't mean they'd have to work on Saturdays. They would simply do what so many other businesses do and employ people who are happy with weekend working.

I went a step further regarding the 'I wouldn't ask people to do something I'm not prepared to do' comment, too. I fly a lot and I love to fly with Virgin Atlantic. However, not once has Richard Branson been there to check in my cases; not once has he offered me a drink or food; never has he shown up to check I'm warm enough and to offer me a blanket. However, although not there personally, he sets the ethos and employs his team to ensure I have a great experience. If he was sitting at home on Necker Island feeling guilty that his team was serving me on a night flight from London to Miami, Virgin would not be the iconic brand that it is. It isn't that Richard wouldn't do this job if he had to. It's that his role in the business is different from the airport team and cabin crew he employs.

When we put it this way, it sounds obvious, but we can still sometimes use the excuse, 'Mine is just a small business, it's not Virgin'. Maybe so. However, it still needs you as the leader. Yes, set a great example because you lead well. But, if you own a nursing home, you don't need to show up every morning to get the residents out of bed – unless you want to.

Your employees are not your friends, doing you a favour by showing up

Remember this: your team members want you to lead. They want you to provide a positive working environment, treat them respectfully, and pay them on time.

Once we had created our dream team, I remember thinking that all my team loved me and wanted to be my friend. However, although we cared about each other – and I had good relationships with most of them – if one of them was to move on and was no longer being employed by me, our relationship ended. When they decided to leave, they left without worrying about me. The fact that I had tried to be a great boss – treating them well, paying them on time, etc. – was long forgotten. One of my regrets was how I had actually spent hours placating and worrying about the team on many, many occasions when I should have been in family time. I missed kids milestones, events, plays, sports fixtures, holidays and playdates – all because the good girl part of me worried what my employees would think. This was stupid. I can never get those times back with my kids.

Please don't make this mistake. Develop your business owner womanpreneur mindset. Let go of the 'good girl' and become an inspiring, empowering leader who runs her business, makes confident decisions – and leads from the front.

Embracing Pollyanna

I was around twelve years old when my mum (who loves me very much) said something that would haunt me for years. We were having a chat where I was being positive about a situation, and she said, 'Well, we can't all be Pollyanna, can we?' At that time, I had no idea what she meant and the conversation just stopped.

Later I looked it up. Who was Pollyanna? Here is a definition from Wikipedia, which is much the same as the one I found:

'The Pollyanna principle or syndrome is the tendency for people to remember pleasant items more accurately than unpleasant ones. Research indicates that at the subconscious level, the mind has a tendency to focus on the optimistic.'

And here's one from the Merriam Webster Dictionary:

'A person characterised by irrepressible optimism and a tendency to find good in everything. Although it is good to be positive and optimistic, unrealistic optimism can be a dangerous syndrome.'

So, back then, I had the first realisation that: OMG! I had a syndrome and it was dangerous!

And from that day, I carried that belief.

I was 'bullied' in a variety of different ways as I grew into a young woman. Not the type of bullying where you're taken behind the bike sheds and beaten up, but I gave my personal power away nonetheless. I allowed others to manipulate me, to take advantage of me and to treat me badly. I didn't stand up for myself. I settled, and was more worried about pleasing others than I was about pleasing myself, because I thought that pleasing myself was selfish and part of my Pollyanna syndrome. I found myself 'not wanting to make a fuss'. I would rather go along with things than say no, in case I upset others, or embarrassed myself at being seen as someone who was not very nice. I allowed people to take advantage and intimidate me, and I would feel guilty a lot. My self-esteem and self-view were not great. And I carried this around with me for years. I allowed it to influence my decisions about my life, relationships and career.

I now realise that my Pollyanna syndrome was not a bad thing – it was an early manifestation of being a Blue Cow. Being a Blue Cow is an awesome thing! So, for any fellow 'Pollyannas' out there, you are awesome! Don't you change one bit, except to take back your personal power. It's your time to shine and if others, including family, friends and colleagues, don't like it, then so what?!

My 'setting-myself-free' moment came during a discussion with my husband in the early days of our relationship. I told him that I suffered with Pollyanna syndrome. He laughed, gave me a big hug, and said, 'Listen to me, you be you! You are the most positive person I know and that's great!' I couldn't believe it! From that day forward, I started to be okay with being positive. I became a Blue Cow, even though I hadn't actually come across her yet. I believe that, in that moment, my husband gave me permission to be me. More importantly, I gave *myself* permission to be me.

I stopped diluting who I was

I became more assertive and stood up for myself in a way I'd never done before

I learnt it was okay to make decisions and move towards the way of life I wanted

I started to feel great about being naturally positive

I appreciated that not everyone would like me for being positive

I decided to be okay with others not liking me, and saying no to people

I decided it was okay to not fit in

If you need 'permission' to be you, here it is:

I GIVE YOU PERMISSION TO SHINE! You are an AWESOME person!

As Eleanor Roosevelt wrote: 'No one can make you feel inferior without your consent.'

Identifying your mindset issues, or 'syndromes'

From working with hundreds of womanpreneurs, it's clear that many of us suffer from a variety of 'syndromes' that hold us back. Most are mindset issues that we can change. What syndromes do you suffer from? Here are a few for you to consider:

- Guilt syndrome
- Rushing woman syndrome
- The I-have-to-do-it-all-myself syndrome
- The I-can't-say-no syndrome
- The I-am-not-enough syndrome
- The lack of self-belief syndrome
- The I-let-people-walk-all-over-me syndrome
- The I-am-bad-with-figures syndrome
- The I-may-get-it-wrong syndrome
- The they-might-not-like-me syndrome

Whatever it is, the first step to overcoming it is to recognise it and acknowledge that whilst it's not your fault – as the 'seed' to your syndrome will have been planted long ago and, in most cases, will have been growing for years – it is your fault if you *choose* to keep it and not overcome it. Especially if it's holding you back.

Letting go of who I thought I was

I remember, from a very young age, thinking I was pretty poor academically. So I made up for it by constantly chatting in class. If I was making everyone laugh, it didn't matter if I wasn't doing well. I remember my primary school teacher telling me I should sit in the corner as I would never finish the green maths book. Everyone else was on orange or red books, which were more advanced than mine, yet I struggled to get anywhere. As there were lots of other kids in the class to teach, the teacher seemed happy to just let me plod along, stuck with the label of 'Miss Green Book'. All the while, I was convincing myself that I wasn't very clever and would never be good at maths. No one told me any different, so that became my belief.

I went through school with this view of myself. So much so that when it came to my GCSE maths many years later, I had this belief so firmly embedded that I wasn't at all surprised when my maths teacher explained that, unlike the rest of my class, I was not even going to be entered into the higher papers. I nodded and agreed. After all, in my head I was still 'Miss Green Book'. I told myself I couldn't do it, my teachers agreed I couldn't do it, so I was destined not to do it. The papers I sat meant that the most I could get was a grade C. It was clear that my teacher thought any grade would be amazing. The results came in and, sure enough, I had managed to get an E in GCSE maths. So, my reality had come true: I was no good at maths!

But this, happily, is not the end of the story. One teacher believed in me, and told me I should retake the paper a few weeks later. I took up the challenge and did retake it, without any other help than this teacher simply telling me I could do it if I believed in myself more. And guess what? I got a C. What a Blue Cow teacher! I am forever grateful to them.

However, my negative self-image was still there, so deep rooted that I thought getting the C must have been a fluke. I spent many years saying, 'I am no good with numbers. I can't do maths, don't ask me about figures.' I felt awful about it – not good enough, not as good as others – and just labelled myself that way. So guess what? Everyone else did too. I had no clue, then, that this persona I had created was not true, that this was not the real me. Or that one day I would play a pivotal role in creating and growing multiple six figure and seven-figure businesses, where I would be in charge of the finances – *and* I would help other people grow their businesses, improve cash flow and get more profit, whilst increasing their net worth.

What beliefs have you carried with you that limit you and allow you (or others) to put yourself down?

I was recently working with a fabulous womanpreneur who has a great business that she started from scratch. In one discussion, we were talking about cash flow and the breakeven of her business and she told me that her business partner (who happens to be her boyfriend) would not show her the figures because he said she would not understand them! Rather than believing in herself – and saying that if she was showed *how* to understand them, she was more than capable – she had settled, and allowed herself to be disempowered. Once I reminded her that she needed to know the figures, and she could do it, she went back and insisted that she was shown them. When discussing this afterwards, she told me she felt amazing and proud of herself for not settling anymore. In fact, she told me she 'put on her high heels, turned and walked away proudly' from that meeting. I could have cried! I loved seeing her confident and shining. This is why I love empowering womanpreneurs to believe in themselves and lose the negative self-image and emotional baggage that holds many of us back.

Loving ourselves

To get emotionally free, we need to love ourselves more. I used to think that was all nonsense. Love myself more, blah! However, once I did start working on myself, I realised that I didn't actually love myself much at all. I was waiting for approval and love from others to feel good about myself. This is a nightmare if you are a boss looking to be loved by the people you are employing! If we are, then the decisions we make and the actions we take are likely to result from our wanting to feel liked, as opposed to what the business needs from us. We have to work on loving ourselves enough so that we do not need the approval of others, which is not easy.

When my kids ask things like, 'Do you think I look nice in this?' or 'Do you think I can do this?', I make sure to say, 'Yes, I do. But, more importantly, do *you* think you look nice in that or do *you* think you can do that?' I want them to take control of how they feel about themselves and use their inner compass to guide them, not seek approval from others in the same way I did.

So many of us feel loved only once we get approval from others. But if we top up our own 'love tank', we don't have to wait for others to keep us fuelled. The more we love ourselves, the more we can serve others and feel good about ourselves in the process. And the more we see ourselves positively, the better leaders and womanpreneurs we will be.

Self-image

What do you think about yourself?

I was recently running a team training day with some clients and the team was discussing their behavioural style at work. We use this to work out how the team members behave and how best to communicate with them. They had completed the DISC profile form (a form of 'psychometric' testing that determines behavioural style at work) and each one had established their personality profile. Then, one awesome lady said, 'I have a problem with one of the words on the form.' I asked which word it was, and she said, '"Outspoken". I don't want to be outspoken.'

Her team (who clearly thought she was a Blue Cow) started jumping in and saying, 'You are outspoken, but not in a bad way. We love how you don't always agree, but you do it nicely.'

The lady responded, 'That word has a negative connotation for me.'

Everyone looked perplexed, until I explained to them that the negative connotation did not come from the here and now. In my view, this lady must have experienced something in her past, maybe even when she was a small child, where she may have given her opinion and it was greeted with, 'You are outspoken', perhaps in a negative way. Maybe she was made 'wrong' by someone and that formed an 'anchor', so now she saw being outspoken as a negative thing, even though everyone else in the room saw it as a great thing.

The team and I discussed how every single person we meet has such 'anchors', whether it's a word, a phrase or a look, which may evoke an emotion, a feeling or a meaning that we created years before. It's not real but it came from how we interpreted that particular situation at the time. We didn't ask the lady about what had happened, but I could tell from her tears that we must have touched on something. In fact, the moment was so emotional I had to hold back tears myself. I hope that session helped her see why she had that negative connotation and how she could now let it go and create a new meaning for the word 'outspoken', based on all the good feedback she'd received from her Blue Cow peers, who encouraged her positively.

Stop keeping yourself small

The world needs you to show up and be you! It needs you to launch your product or service confidently and grow your business so you can reach as many people as possible. You have to stop holding yourself back, believing your own negative, brown cow voice. If you don't change, then the very people who need your product, service, message or outcome won't gain access to you and the awesome thing your business sells. Consider this:

'What great thing would you attempt if you knew you could not fail?'

Robert Schuller

It's time to step the hell up and get it done! Are you keeping yourself small, limiting yourself? Are you not being as visible as you should be because of fear, or stress over what others will think? Well, your worry about not being good enough isn't empowering you, and it's time for that to stop! You deserve a business and life you love. You can make a massive impact in this world. Stop worrying about the brown cow 'haters'. You're not doing this for them! You're doing this for you and all the people you love, to whom you want to give a better life, as well as all the people who need your service and product who will benefit from your business.

Mummy guilt

'Mummy guilt' used to really hold me back. If I was working, I felt guilty that I should be with my kids; if I was with my kids, I felt guilty that I should be at work. I know this is a common problem amongst mums in business. As our family started to grow, I found it really hard to balance being a great mummy with running my business. I seemed to be constantly trying to do both roles at the same time.

Eventually, I realised that the best thing I could be for my kids was the most inspired and happy version of myself. This would stop the grumpy, overtired version from rearing its ugly head. So, I set myself some rules. What were the most important elements of being a great mummy on my terms? I decided I would design my business to run so that I could achieve these. This meant I would stop trying to do everything, and concentrate on the things that mattered most to me.

I wanted to:

- Do the school runs 90% of the time. So, I decided to set all my meetings and events to start after 9.30am so I didn't have to rush
- Do the bedtime routine: homework, bath and story, cuddles and snuggles. So, I designed my business hours so that I could always do this, even if it meant I went back to work afterwards to hit a deadline
- Be able to attend any school events (sports days, music shows, plays, etc.) that I wished
- Take my kids to as many parties as possible or, if I was away on business, enlist help so that they didn't miss out
- Take my kids to some of my business events and trips and expose them to positive personal development

I would put a limit on:

- Working on weekends (unless it could absolutely not be avoided)
- Answering my work phone during family time
- Using my social media whilst with kids (or only when strictly necessary)

What about you? What would be your most important 'rules' for being a great mummy, as a Blue Cow womanpreneur? What do you need to change in your business or working life to achieve this?

My next question is: how soon can you change it? When answering, bear in mind how quickly time flies. People used to tell me this. I now look at my older kids (currently 14 and 13) and, whilst they still need me, they certainly don't want me hanging around in their lives in the way they used to (when I was probably trapped in my previous business and couldn't always give them the mummy time they needed and deserved). We can always do more business, but we cannot do more 'kids' childhood' once it has passed.

These are the good old days

Have you ever heard someone say, 'Ah, those were the good old days?' when reflecting on aspects of their earlier life? My husband and I were trying to have a catch-up chat as we had not seen each other properly for a few days – he had been working away – and we ended up discussing how messy and noisy our house was. It was a particularly 'hectic' weekend with lots of kids over for playdates, all ages, taking over all different rooms. There was laughter, arguments, requests for pizza and ice-cream, interruptions, dogs barking, etc. Then, as he and I started to grumble a little about wanting some peace, we stopped, catching ourselves. It was then that we had the realisation that these days – the choatic, busy, life-filled days – are, in fact, 'the good old days' about which we will reminisce when we are old (fingers crossed we make it, as I don't take getting old for granted).

So what about you? Are the days you have the opportunity to live *right now* going to be the times that you look back on as the good old days? Will you look back and have lots of happy memories or will you simply remember feeling stressed, trapped, or feeling a lack of joy. You get to decide how you create the days that will become your 'good old days'. Don't miss them because you allowed yourself to be constantly stressed or unfulfilled.

Fear

This is a *moosive* mindset issue that stops us in our tracks. However, so often the word 'fear' can mean:

False **E**motion **A**ppearing **R**eal

Basically, we need to remind ourselves that the fears and worries we often focus on *aren't real!* They are made up by our brain and mostly delivered through the brown cow voice that bombards us with negative thoughts, instead of encouraging us. Fear is something that stops many womanpreneurs from having it all. We spend our time needlessly worrying and fearful – what a waste of energy! Imagine if I told you that I drive my car every day worrying that a giant bear is going to jump out in front of me. Instead of looking at the beautiful countryside, I am focusing on the bear. I do this repeatedly – and yet the bear never comes!

My six-year-old daughter came running into my bedroom shouting that she was scared. When I asked what she was scared of she became hysterical and told me she was frightened of the fly in her room. She was too scared to go in there. When I asked her why, she could not give me a logical answer. She said, ' I just am scared'. As the conversation went on, she explained that the fly was not even alive, it was lying dead in the corner.

After I removed the fly, we talked about fear and how we sometimes worry about things that may never happen or just worry and feel fearful with no real reason why. Ensure you are not living day to day being worried about 'the dead fly' – something that is imagined, or that may never happen. If you are allowing it to hold you back, maybe all you need to do is to take a simple action to remove it.

Everyone feels fear. Everyone has doubt. What matters is what we do with those feelings.

If you find yourself fearful, start by reading the awesome book *Feel the Fear and Do It Anyway* by Susan Jeffers. Then consider, logically, what you are actually fearful of. When I ask my womanpreneur clients to do this, these are the fears they mention:

- Being a failure
- Not being good enough
- What people will think
- Losing it all
- Rejection
- Having no money

Yet, realistically, all these are things you *could* deal with if they happened. In fact, some of them provide the best business lessons ever. If you were to lose it all, what action would you take? Most of us would feel sorry for ourselves for a bit, then our inner Blue Cow would call to us and we'd start again, but this time using the lessons learnt from that experience. If we were really desperate we would get a job whilst we healed and started again. In my own experience, and what I've gathered from speaking to womanpreneurs all around the world, the challenging times are the ones that have taught us the most. I know people sometimes hate to hear this, especially if they are in the middle of a challenging time, but it is true. So stop living in fear, get out there and just do your best. Remember this awesome Franklin D. Roosevelt quote: 'A smooth sea never made a skilled sailor'.

Be okay with making decisions

Many womanpreneurs are scared to make decisions. Maybe it is the fear of being wrong and making a mistake. When asked their opinion, they settle. I have a friend who, when we go out for dinner, always replies to my question, 'Do you want a curry?' with, 'If you like'. It frustrates me, and I say, 'It's not if *I* like. I am asking you! Do *you* like?'

I used to find it really hard to make decisions. When we moved into our new house ten years ago, I knew I wanted carpets, but my husband wanted floorboards. I didn't say anything, and he went about sanding the floorboards and working really hard to make them nice. Four years later, we were having a discussion and I told him, 'I hate floorboards. I much prefer carpets.' He said he didn't care either way and why had I not said anything before? My answer was that I had been worried that if I had chosen the carpets I would have chosen wrongly. And then we would have spent all that money, resulting in neither of us ending up liking them.

He laughed and said, 'Well, if that happened I am sure we could have saved up and you could have chosen a different one and just replaced it.'

But it wasn't even about the money, it was about the decision. Here I was, a successful womanpreneur, but I was putting up with floorboards I hated because I was worried about making the wrong decision when it came to the choice of a carpet. Can you relate to this? Are there areas in your life that you know you need to make a decision about but are putting off? The lesson here is, you can always make a different decision if you are unhappy with the previous one. (Thank you, Steve, for helping me with this!)

Letting go of 'comparitis'

Comparing ourselves to others is something we all do, and it holds us back. Comparitis is a concept developed by Leon Festinger in 1954. Social comparison means we determine our own self-worth based on how we compare ourselves to other people. This leads to our constantly evaluating ourselves across various aspects of our personal and social life (looks, wealth, success, etc.)

Most people usually compare themselves by looking at people whom they consider to be either below or above their skill set or circumstances. This is called upward or downward comparison. Downward comparison is when we have a difficult situation in our own life but make ourselves feel better by thinking, 'Well, today was bad but at least my life isn't as bad as Doris's at the moment.' This makes us feel better (although it's not so great for Doris).

Upward comparisons can actually make us feel better, but sometimes worse. Normally, we tend to use upward comparisons with people whom we consider to be 'better than we are' in, perhaps, an ability, social standing, appearance or talent. When we make this kind of comparison, we often end up feeling bad about ourselves. However, for some womanpreneurs, it can actually make us want to improve and get better.

I used to suffer from comparitis quite badly. (If I'm really honest, sometimes I still do.) I would look at others, judging and comparing all sorts of things, which often ended up with me feeling pretty bad and less than good enough. Things that included:

- Qualifications
- Career progression
- Size and weight
- Public speaking
- Success levels
- Popularity

You name it, I could compare it. And I was really good at putting myself down, often coming to the conclusion I was not as good. Have you ever done this?

Comparitis would leave me feeling down, frustrated, deflated and irritated at myself. It wasn't that I wanted the other person to fail, be less successful or look less gorgeous. It was rather that I would get cross with myself because I thought I should be better, further ahead, or whatever my point of comparison was. I would then start putting myself down, both in my head and out loud.

If you are focusing on your business competition or what other people are doing, you are never going to achieve your dreams, be successful on your terms or set yourself free! Be the best version of yourself. Create the best business and life you can and stop wasting time comparing. Put your energy and attention into your passion.

Stay in your lane

Woah! They are powerful emotional-freedom words. Simple yet profound. If you stay in your lane, the comparitis stops. My husband taught me this, which I've used with hundreds of my clients since. Imagine the Olympic swimmer. When racing, they have to swim their own race, focusing on their own goal at the end of the pool. If they spend their time looking around watching what others are doing, they remove the focus from their intention. If they don't swim their own race, they are never going to win.

So stay in your lane. Stop comparing yourself to others. The only time it's productive to compare is if you see someone doing something you want to do, and you ask them to show you how to do it too. And if you notice you are feeling bad looking at what other people are doing, perceiving it to be better than what you are doing, then raise your game. Put your energy and passion into becoming better at the thing you want to achieve. This is a much better use of your time and energy. After all, all our emotions were created for a purpose. Jealousy has a positive use if we only make sure to use the em*otion as a spring*board to improve our lives for the better.

Other 'excuses' that keep us from being emotionally free:

- I don't have the qualifications. Many other womanpreneurs don't either. If you need specific qualifications, go and get them. However, you may not even need them.
- I am too young or too old. This is just a lie you are telling yourself. You are never too young or too old to create a business or life you love.
- I am too fat or too skinny. If *you* think you are too fat, then set

about losing some weight (please note I have put an accent on the word 'you'). If you think you are too skinny, ensure you are wearing clothes you feel great in (more about this later).

- I don't have enough money to do that. This is one that really frustrates me. I recently posted in a group about the importance of not settling in your business. I was talking about service-based businesses where customers visit your premises, where you shouldn't have dirty carpets and wallpaper hanging off the wall. One lady replied that she would love to make changes but was 'skint'. Being skint is not a reason for not taking action. If you do not have enough money, you simply need a plan to get some. The absence of a plan means you will always be 'skint'.

Add any other limiting beliefs you may have as to why you cannot achieve what you want in business and life and consider how you can change your beliefs and what actions you can take. Whatever you come up with, I can guarantee someone else has experienced the same, and overcome it to become successful and happy. You can too.

The most important letter you will ever write

In order to help yourself become emotionally free, you're going to write a letter. This is a private letter to yourself that only you will read. In the letter, you're going to:

- Tell yourself you are awesome and how much you love yourself
- Forgive yourself if you need to
- Tell yourself it's okay to stop feeling guilty about anything that happened in the past
- Tell yourself it's time to remove any labels that are holding you back
- Tell yourself that you're exactly where you're supposed to be right now – you should *not* be further ahead, more successful, etc.
- Tell yourself you can do whatever it is you want – you are smart enough, brave enough, and can do it

- Tell yourself anything else you know you need to hear that will help you move forward emotionally.

Once you've written it, read it through – perhaps even destroy it if you want to. The idea is that we spend a little bit of time giving ourselves some of the self-love that many of us need but didn't have as a child. Self-love that we don't usually allow ourselves as adults.

Womanpreneur

'Reset Moment'

- Do you have beliefs that are holding you back?
- Can you relate to any of the syndromes I've highlighted?
- Do you need to change your 'inner circle'? Do you need to stop being someone else to please people who are acting like brown cows? If so, take action. Take back your power! Unleash your inner Blue Cow!
- What are you not doing in your life that you want to do but may have been persuaded not to?
- How are you holding yourself back from having the life and business you want (and deserve)?

3
SELF-CARE

'Health care and self-care are not a luxury – they are a necessity.'

JO DAVISON

The third step in the R.E.S.E.T formula is self-care.

Self-care is made up of:

1. How we treat ourselves, including all aspects that affect our health and happiness
2. How we allow others to treat us, including all aspects that involve our peer group and relationships we have with others

Are you happy?

A few years ago, I met up with a colleague, by chance, whom I had not seen for many years. We chatted about business and life and she asked me the question, 'Are you happy?' I replied that yes I was, and started sharing a few aspects of my life I was happy with. As the conversation went on, I had the realisation that I may have appeared to be showing off when this hadn't been my intention at all, I had simply been answering the question. I found myself 'dumbing' down my answer to ensure I did not appear 'up myself'. Afterwards, I thought a lot about that question and why I felt the need to not appear too happy. Everyone deserves happiness. Whilst we cannot control what life throws at us and we cannot be happy all the time, our life should be full of happiness.

I began to ask my clients the question and was surprised at the results. Some womanpreneurs, who appeared successful, motivated and driven, started to cry when I asked them this question. Many told me stories of being unhappy, many felt powerless to control their happiness. You deserve to be happy. You deserve a happy life. You are allowed to live happily, so be sure you remember this when you are designing your life. The one person in charge of whether you live a happy life is you.

Being in charge of our health and happiness

The way we look after ourselves today is going to have an impact on our tomorrow. Many womanpreneurs I meet tell me that they don't:

- Have time to exercise
- Eat regularly
- Eat healthily
- Sleep well
- Take time to relax
- Spend time chilling out with friends
- Don't laugh often

Many tell me they are:

- Stressed
- Worn out
- Rushing about a lot
- Smoking
- Drinking too much alcohol
- Experiencing pain – physical or emotional
- Feeling depressed

The people who are reporting this are not employees with bad bosses; they are womanpreneurs who are their own boss. We went into business to serve through our product and service, yes, but also so that we could have more freedom and choice. Many of us who wanted to rid ourselves of our old boss have simply replaced him or her with a terrible boss that works us even harder: ourselves! For many womanpreneurs, self-care is horribly low on their priority list.

If we don't make a determined effort to prioritise looking after our health and treat our bodies respectfully, they will shut us down, forcing us to make a change. This is exactly what happened to me and I know it has happened to many womanpreneurs.

My body forced me to change

It was a Friday lunchtime. I had been to the gym and was on my way back to work to make client calls. I'd had a stressful morning already as there had been a challenge at school: all the kids except mine had turned up with a costume for their school play rehearsal. I left my eldest daughter sobbing at school while I rushed home to 'put together something', before heading back to school to deliver it so I wouldn't feel like the worst mum ever. Now, I am the world's least likely person to be able to put together a suitable costume, but I knew I couldn't let my daughter down. I was already late for a gym session with my personal trainer and, afterwards, I had back-to-back client calls to make.

I'd been feeling tired, but nothing too bad, and I wasn't feeling stressed as such – just very busy. My head started to ache on the drive home and I assumed it was because I'd done some pretty heavy exercise at the gym. But by the time I got home, it was banging, and in the shower my eyes started to go blurry. Whilst preparing for my calls on my laptop, I noticed that the words 'went funny'. Although I had written them, I couldn't understand what they meant.

At about this time, my husband happened to call me and, when I explained my symptoms, he told me to go straight to A&E. We both have clinical backgrounds and, although that sometimes makes us a bit neurotic, in this case it was clear that something potentially sinister was happening. I never got headaches and was rarely unwell.

However, I had client calls booked and I hate letting people down. So, I decided to do the calls lying on the floor in my office with my headset on, and let my clients do the talking. That way, at least the calls got done. (Please note: whilst some of you may think this is stupid – which I will admit it was – I know others will completely understand where I am coming from here!)

Just before my first call, my left arm and leg went numb, and my hand felt weak. Then, suddenly, I felt like I'd been hit on the back of the head with a hammer. Luckily, I was able to crawl to the sofa just outside my office and shout to my mum, who was at my house at the time. She called an ambulance. The paramedics rushed me to hospital and, whilst in the ambulance, I could hear them calling ahead and speaking to doctors. I remember thinking that the person they were talking about sounded *very* poorly.

On arrival at A&E, I was rushed into the back area where I was surrounded by what seemed like huge numbers of medical staff, buzzing around me like bees around a honey pot. They poked and prodded me, asked me what had happened, tested my muscles, touched my face and checked my eyes. It was then that the junior doctor looked at me and said, 'We think you have had a fatal brain haemorrhage.' It was the word 'fatal' that shocked me. It can only mean one thing, and that is DEATH. Having a clinical background – previously having been a nurse in A&E and seen people come in with brain bleeds, as well as having been a chiropractor and medical student – with knowledge of the body, I was very scared. I remember lying there thinking three things – all centred around, 'I can't die!':

- I can't leave my children. They need me
- I can't leave my husband. He needs me
- Don't tell my mum what you think until you've done tests as you'll upset her. (She was in the waiting room on her own, hoping for good news.)

Then everything went black.

When I woke up, I was lying in a hospital room. I was alone. Everything was white and silent. My head still hurt and my arm felt weak, but I could move it. The nurse came in and said that I'd been sleeping and needed to have more tests – including more X-rays,

MRI and CT scans and a lumbar puncture – and I should carry on resting. I felt completely drained, a heaviness I'd never experienced before. After a few days of being bedridden and having lots of tests, I started to feel better and was told that I had *not* had a fatal brain bleed after all. (I'd kind of guessed by then!)

I was told I would be staying in hospital for the foreseeable future whilst they worked out what had happened to me and what treatment would be needed. My husband, meanwhile, had told our children I was on a spa weekend with my best friend. I didn't have to worry about them; he had everything under control. He had also told my clients I was taking time off, and my team was running the business. My mum and mother-in-law reassured me that they were supporting my family.

At the time I simply felt huge relief that I was still alive. Also for the first time in a long time, I only had to think about myself. I literally sobbed and sobbed so hard that I didn't think I could cry any more, and then I would sob again. It went on for two days.

Once I started to feel better, the hospital room and the complete silence within it became like a sanctuary. And I did nothing but rest. During my stay, I had plenty of time to think and I began to see that I had been putting too much energy into certain areas of my life. When I was faced with the 'you may die' conversation, I realised that they were the things that really didn't matter the most. I also realised that the people who mattered the most to me were getting the least of me. I love being in business, but it was clear I wasn't exercising great self-care and my work-life balance was out of kilter. My health, sanity and family were suffering. I was wearing too many hats.

Please don't wait for a health scare or diagnosis before you start making your health and self-care a priority. You should never feel guilty about taking a day off. In fact, if anything, you should actually feel guilty for *not* taking time off. No one can work endlessly and perform at their best without a break. You should never be so arrogant as to think that the world will end if you dare to delegate or put your to-do list on hold for a couple of days. Don't take your health for granted. I used to think that if I wanted something done right, I had to do it myself. I also thought I was invincible. I was wrong. I needed to get better at delegating and empowering others to do a great job and make self-care higher on my priority list.

You have to stop thinking that the business will fall apart if you're not there all the time. If it *is* falling apart, take action to add in better systems and a leadership team. Then let them lead!

I speak to womanpreneurs all the time who say:

- They're worried their business will crumble if they take time off
- Their team won't do as good a job as they themselves can
- They don't earn enough money to take good care of themselves
- They don't have time to exercise

I used to think all these things! However, that attitude and those beliefs were not serving me, they were killing me. If we don't take care of ourselves, we will, at best, end up burned out and, at worst, face an early death. My health scare made me re-evaluate my health care and self-care, and I made the necessary changes to rectify the situation. One simple decision I made was to limit my work at weekends so I could be the mummy and wife I wanted to be. The 'old' me would never have done this. I will share more about this later in the book when we talk about the 'womanpreneur business owner voyage'.

Don't take tomorrow for granted

At a similar time to my own health scare, a good friend of mine, Laura, passed away suddenly with meningitis. It was another reminder to ensure my self-care and health goals were a priority. One minute

Laura and I were chatting about our lives and businesses and all the things we were going to create in the next twelve months. She was a 29-year-old beautiful soul with big dreams. Next she was dead, leaving behind two young children and a lovely husband. Laura left a lasting legacy with me to make every day count, as we never know when our time will be up. What matters most to Laura's kids? Her business empire that she ran or the memories of what a great mum she was, a positive shining light in their lives and the lives of many others? Don't be so busy making a business that you forget to make a life. Don't say, 'Tomorrow I will be a better mummy, wife, partner, etc.' ... because our tomorrows are not guaranteed. Make those memories today.

The voice in our head

We hear this voice constantly every day. Is it a blue cow voice that bigs you up or a brown cow voice that puts you down? Do you wake up and look in the mirror and say, 'Hello, you gorgeous, awesome lady?' Or do you tell yourself something negative. If an opportunity presents itself, do you tell yourself to go for it or do you put yourself down and stop yourself from having a go? Do you allow yourself to see the negative in situations and dwell in that place? If so, it's time to stop it. Positive self-care means empowering yourself to feel good about yourself.

You are a unique, awesome, fabulous, gorgeous human. Your being here on this planet is not a mistake. You were created to contribute your ideas, and all aspects of your being to others, and your being in it makes the world a better place! You have to believe this. You are enough to achieve *whatever* you want ... if you let yourself!

Our thoughts and self-care hugely impact the quality of our lives. Two people could be in the same situation but have a completely different view of it. Imagine it's a rainy day. One person might be complaining about it, the other rejoicing because there is a beautiful rainbow. Or they may live in a place where rain is a luxury; they're desperate for some to grow crops to feed their family. We cannot control *what* happens to us, but we can control how we *respond* to what happens to us. So start bigging yourself up. EVERY DAY! This does not mean you have to become arrogant, just self confident.

Managing stress

I recently saw a post in my women in business community Facebook group where someone had asked, 'What is the best cure for stress?' Lots of our awesome members had offered ideas and suggestions. However, let's be clear, the best *cure* for stress is to *stop* running your business and life in a way that makes you stressed! A little bit of stress can be good, especially if it motivates you positively. However, lots of stress, constantly being under pressure, feeling sweaty, flustered, rushing about constantly, not sleeping, and feeling out of control are all signs that you MUST take action to stop. You can! I did.

I could do 'stressed out, rushing woman' really well. By being this way, I was disempowering myself, thinking this was how successful women lived. Women who were not constantly working or stressed could not achieve as much, I thought, and therefore were not as successful. This is BROWN COW THINKING. Stop thinking that someone else is in charge of you, your life and business. Change your mindset and routine.

Take care of your body. If you don't, where else are you going to live?

Chiropractic changed my life. I believe everyone should have it as a part of their life and wellbeing plan. It all began for me when I damaged my knee on the netball court and had to have it reconstructed. Recovery was very slow and I saw every healthcare practitioner, but no one could help me. My pain level was high and my mobility was low. To cut a long story short, I ended up going to watch a netball game (as I couldn't play, but would still go and support my team) and there I met a lady who was a chiropractor. We ended up discussing my knee and she said she could help. I was very skeptical as I had already seen tons of healthcare practitioners, but she was very persuasive and I ended up booking a consultation. After a few sessions, not only was my pain gone, but I was able to get back to work – and, most importantly at that time, back to playing netball. I continued seeing my chiropractor and discovered chiropractic could help much more than dodgy knees. I found my period pain, back pain, headaches and hayfever were all helped massively. I found it so inspiring, I returned to university to do a degree in chiropractic.

Chiropractic is not just about helping bad backs, it is a healthcare system that uses adjustments to keep the body functioning optimally. Although many people only go when they are in pain, many go when they are feeling good and want to stay that way. I get adjusted every week, as do my husband, kids and loved ones. I no longer see patients myself, however I am still a raving fan and if you have not had a chiropractic check-up, I strongly urge you to do so. Ensure you see someone who is registered as this means they will have done a four- or five-year degree specialising in the nervous system and will be well qualified to help keep your nerves and joints functioning well. You can find an amazing Chiropractor by posting in my free Blue Cow Women in Business FB group: www.facebook.com/groups/bluecowwomeninbusiness/

As well as seeing the chiropractor, I would love you to consider having regular massage. This is not only great for keeping your muscles spasm free, and loosening off tension, it is also great to ensure you get time out, a short time where you can relax and recharge. Time away from business, internet, clients, laptops, kids calling 'Muuummmm', partners, and everyone else. I have an awesome massage therapist, Sara, who comes to my house every week. Look into doing this too. (If a brown cow voice in your head is mooing right now about finding the money, we will discuss later how you can create the abundance to afford it).

Another healthcare system I love is Chinese Medicine and acupuncture. When we wanted to get pregnant with our third child, I was 38 years old. I had some medical tests and was pretty much told that my eggs were 'old', my egg reserve was very low, and there was little hope of my getting pregnant. I was devastated. I knew I was very lucky, as I already had two amazing boys, but when people would tell me, 'Never mind, at least you have two kids,' it didn't make my urge for a third child feel any less. I would think about it all the time and I found myself feeling really down about it. When I researched online, I found that not only could chiropractic help with getting pregnant (I was already having that), but Chinese Medicine and acupuncture could help too. I booked an appointment with an amazing lady called Catherine Huang who specialised in fertility and pregnancy. Within three months of seeing her, despite having been told there was little chance by the medical doctor, I got pregnant and went on to have my first daughter. I was 38 then, but was totally surprised when I fell pregnant again naturally at 43, and went on to have our fourth child, another healthy daughter. So the message is, don't always believe what the doctors tell you, when we improve our self-care and free ourselves emotionally, miracles do happen! (However, a warning: you need to make time for sex every two or three days. It's amazing how many busy super-couples go to fertility clinics, only to admit their working life hardly ever allows time for it ...) You can reach Catherine Huang here: http://www.catherinehuang-acupuncture.co.uk/

I still have acupuncture for general health and wellbeing. Prevention, after all, is better than cure. All these healthcare choices require an investment as they are not free. However what better investment is there than your health? After all, if you didn't have your health, think for a moment what and who would suffer. Yes your business might, but, more importantly, your loved ones would – the very people who mean the most. Just because we didn't make looking after ourselves a priority. If you won't do it for yourself, take care of yourself for them.

Exercise

For years I told myself that I was too busy to exercise. This went on and on, and at one point I was paying a gym membership every month but *never* going. (I hear tons of womanpreneurs admit that they do this). One day I was returning home from a business consultation visit in London. I found myself at a tube station where the lift was broken and the only option was to climb a spiral staircase that had *hundreds* of stairs. Halfway up I was so exhausted, I actually sat down on the step and had a panic that I was going to die, alone and on the tube staircase. After a rest and giving myself a strong talking to, I made it to the top, disgusted with myself for not being fitter. If I felt like this at my current age, what would happen in 20 years' time? Returning home, I decided to do something about it. I knew the gym option wasn't going to work for me. If I didn't exercise in the morning, I knew the day would take over and, before I knew it, it would be time to collect the kids and I would have missed the exercise window.

At this time, I also wanted to lose some weight and I was recommended David King's Fat Shocker programme. I loved the programme, although it was pretty brutal: you had to exercise every day. At first I thought there was no way I would have time, but David was tough and said I had to make the time. He suggested I get an exercise bike, put it by my bed and do a ride early in the morning before the kids woke up and I had to start getting them ready. When he told me this, I actually laughed – there was no way I wanted to do that! However, it didn't take me long to realise that it would be a great way of fitting in exercise, and it worked brilliantly well. Every morning, without fail, I would get on the bike and do a 30-minute class (via the internet) before my shower and getting the kids up. I could then spend the day feeling rather smug and pleased with myself. I am currently on a break, after giving birth, but look forward to getting started again. Amy, an awesome personal trainer friend of mine, tells me that I should also consider doing three sessions a week of HIIT (high intensity interval training) of around 20 – 30 minutes each. She tells me it's a great calorie burner and it will boost my metabolism. Amy encourages us all that 30 mins of exercise, even for the busiest of womanpreneurs, is achievable and effective. Don't be put off by the thought of 60 – 90 minutes in the gym – get the job done with a shorter, more intense session that will leave you buzzing. We can all prioritise 30 minutes! Thanks Amy! If you need help or advice, you can get hold of her here www.zonefitnessessex.co.uk.

So you think you have not got time for exercise, change your mindset. Set your alarm earlier, get a stationary bike, and set a goal to ride it first thing every morning. You will be glad you did. Exercise is a great stress reliever as well as getting us fit. If you cannot bear the stationary bike, set a daily time to walk or run around the block. Any exercise is better than none. Get a PT like Amy. Choosing whether to exercise or not is a choice. Don't blame lack of time. I joke with my clients that I had time to eat the cake and drink the wine, but I had to make time to get rid of the calories. Don't think you don't have time, think *HOW can I make the time?*

It's okay to admit when you need a little help

As a womanpreneur, we often see asking for help and being vulnerable as a weakness. This is a brown cow view. Every woman, at times, needs help and support; we simply cannot do everything. It took me a long time to agree with this, feeling that, as a strong woman, I could handle anything and everything. I know many of us feel the same. I still think this, yet now I know that it is a strength to ask for help. It is especially important on the 'not so good' days, which every single one of us has now and again (or more if we are brave enough to admit it).

An awesome client of mine recently arrived at one of my mastermind events and, although she was present physically, I could tell something was wrong. When I went to connect with her in the break, she revealed that she'd been feeling so low she thought her husband, kids and business would be better off if she jumped in front of the train on her way home later that day. OMG!

This lady is beautiful, successful, determined and a real Blue Cow womanpreneur. You would never imagine that she could ever think this way. I reassured her that she was not alone (sadly, I have heard this lots of times) and immediately insisted that she see a doctor for some help. Although we had a plan to alter her business and life situation so that the source of her unhappiness could change, we needed to change how she saw herself. She needed some external help – and that's okay! Taking responsibility and asking for help is positive. The next step is to take action to change the things in our lives that are making us unhappy, rather than staying in the negative place. If you are finding yourself drinking too much alcohol and/or relying on sleeping pills, anti-anxiety medicines, or other drugs to help you get through the day-to-day, it is valuable to seek outside help to identify those life issues that may be underlying your symptoms.

Thank goodness this lady spoke to me and took action, or the outcome – not only for her but also her husband and gorgeous kids – could have been very different. When I needed help to break long-held patterns and get rid of old beliefs, I saw an amazing hypnotherapist called Alice Pinion. Alice used the 'Thrive' technique created by Rob Kelly. We started by looking at whether I was being led by an internal (self) locus of control or an external (outside) locus of control. At the time, it was clear that I was being led much more by the external. Alice helped me see how this was not serving me.

The process I went through with Alice was very effective for me. It was as if I had arrived in her office, and imaginary cupboards were bulging with issues, limiting beliefs and worries that I needed to deal with, but was either too scared or too busy to do so. The imaginary cupboard doors were about to pop open at any minute but I still ignored them. She helped me to 'open the cupboard doors', allowing all the negative thoughts, experiences, guilt, worry, fear and doubt to tumble out. We then dealt with each thing individually. It was painful at times, with lots of tears and laughter, but extremely liberating. If you haven't had a good old, emotional, 'imaginary cupboard' clear-out, I strongly recommend you do. If you can see Alice, then even better! She is awesome. There is no excuse, you can contact her here www.alicepinion.co.uk. Tell her I sent you!

What are your health goals?

We are planting the seeds for our future health right now. It's a daily choice we make. However, some people only think about their health when it's threatened. There was a time when I can honestly say my health was not high on my list of priorities. I would tell myself I didn't have time to exercise and eat healthily. Mentally, I put myself under constant pressure to be more, do more, achieve more – and I never felt I was achieving enough. I took it for granted that good health would always be with me.

What does good health mean to you? Look at this list and grade yourself out of 10 as to the importance you give to each item in your life, 1 being not much and 10 being a lot. Then ask yourself what level of importance you are giving your health right now.

- Exercise
- Nutrition
- Wellbeing
- Time out
- Stress relief

- Recharge time
- Days off
- Date nights
- Friends time
- Walks in nature
- Fun
- Wasting time

Now write down what you need to make time for and decide when you are going to fit these things into your day-to-day life. I used to think going for a massage or a facial were luxuries, and would often feel guilty about having them, as there was so much else on my to-do list. However, then I realised it was much better for my husband, my kids, my clients, and everyone who came into contact with me if I was looking after myself. If my health was poor, I wouldn't be the person they all needed me to be and, ultimately, the person I deserved to be.

Womanpreneurs need to take their health goals seriously (just as seriously as their business goals!).

Surround yourself with Blue Cows

As we said at the start of this chapter, self-care involves how we look after ourselves but it also involves who we spend time with and how we allow others to treat us. Caring about ourselves means that we cannot allow ourselves to be around people who do not help us feel empowered. This isn't easy, however building a business and happy life is hard enough without having 'brown cow naysayers' in your life.

'People's lives are a direct reflection of the expectations of their peer group. If your peer group doesn't expect much, it's just a matter of time before you lower your expectations of yourself.'

Anthony Robbins

Take a piece of paper, draw yourself in the middle and then draw six circles around yourself. In the circle closest to you, write the names of all the people with whom you spend the most time. Now look at the names. Do these people support you? Do they allow you to be you, encourage you, bring light into your life? Or do they put you down, discourage you, zap your life force?

Next, put the names of other people in your life in the other circles and do the same exercise. Look at your circles of names. Are these people Blue Cows? Did you know that we become like the five people we hang out with the most? So, who are you hanging out with?

Unfortunately, you may look at those names and have the realisation that those in your 'inner circle' are not actually those who encourage you the most. Some of those may be people you cannot 'remove' from your life. However, you *can* change how often you see them and, when you do see them, how you allow yourself to act and feel around them. I hear people say, 'So-and-so made me feel like XYZ', and this just isn't true because 'so-and-so' can't make us feel anything. We decide how we feel in response to situations and people. So, if we allow ourselves to feel down, bullied, put down, etc. around these people, we are the ones who must be brave enough to change.

When I made the decision to do this, I found that some people didn't like it. In fact, they preferred the people-pleasing version of me, who put up with their negative behaviour towards me. I felt so guilty at first. As anyone who has been trained into being a 'good girl' knows, when you break free, the person you are breaking free from doesn't like it. They can be aggressive, nasty, spread horrible rumours, slag you off to others, play the victim so you appear like the bad person. They do this because they hope you will then revert back to your former self, return to them and be under their control again. For me, ultimately, I had to remove those people from my life or only let them in on my terms. It was scary and I felt guilty. However, I knew I could never be the person I wanted and was destined to be if I carried on being that same person surrounded by those same people. If you know this will be the same for you, please believe you will be okay. Once you make the decision not to have brown cowness in the people around you, you will find being a leader in your business and life much easier.

Your life partner

Who you choose as your life partner (and who chooses you as theirs) is going to *hugely* impact your life and business. Why is it that so many women (and men) are in unhappy relationships? Ask yourself the question: am I happy? There have been many, many occasions when I have spoken to women about their relationships and they tell me they are unhappy. In some cases, they tell me about situations that are so awful, it is not surprising they are miserable, and that makes me very sad. It's hard not to feel frustrated, however, if I see one of those same awesome ladies again and she tells me that things have not changed and she is still unhappy. She is guilty of settling.

You deserve to live your life alongside someone who is your biggest raving fan. Someone who loves you: meaning they support you, encourage you, are positive to you and about you, treat you kindly, share with you, and are committed to you. They want to see you 'win' at the game of life. Equally and very importantly, the life partner you choose deserves that same love and support from you, too. Anything less – including meanness, bullying, violence, putting the other down – is not acceptable behaviour in a loving relationship from either partner. When I was younger I wasn't always a Blue Cow in my relationships. I would get into moods that could last days and I wasn't always as kind as I could have been. Looking back, this was probably due to my own lack of self-esteem and my self-doubt. I realised that there was only one person in my relationship who could ultimately make me happy, and that was me. I had to stop trying to control the other person and expect them to 'top up my love tank'. I am the only person who can do that, and the responsibility is mine.

My husband and I have a great relationship. I am not saying that to 'show off' and I am not claiming we are the world's most perfect couple. Like anyone, we have to continually work at our relationship. Especially as we have four kids, two dogs, multiple businesses and busy lives. However we are happy, and the thing is, we made a decision to be happy together. What I mean is that we literally sat down and agreed that we would be each other's best supporter; we would not get in moods, we would talk through challenges, we would never slam doors, walk out, swear at each other, go to bed without saying goodnight. We both told each other how we wanted to be treated and what made us feel loved. We discussed our roles at home and in the businesses that we have together. Then we continue to uphold our agreement. We asked ourselves: are we committed to staying together and to love each other? And we both said yes. Do we irritate each other sometimes? Yes, of course – we are human! However, we try to show up as the best version of ourselves. Maintaining a great relationship takes commitment from both partners. We can never take the other person for granted.

Self-care means not settling for a life partner who treats you badly and not being a bad partner to someone else. Remember, too, that self-care means caring enough about ourselves to not let others abuse us, whether physically or emotionally. We all deserve better than this. If we are staying in a negative situation that doesn't serve us positively, and expecting it to change, we must extricate ourselves from it.

It's much harder to create a life you love and the six- or seven-figure business you deserve if you are allowing yourself to be with the wrong life partner. I appreciate every couple has ups and downs, but if it is more than a few ups and downs, maybe it is time to leave. I appreciate how easy that is to say and how hard it is to do. But if you don't, you are wasting your life living unhappily; things will never get better unless you both want them to. I realise that if you have children this makes decision-making especially hard, but it is never in a child's interest having to watch parents being mean to each other, or stuck in a loveless, violent or controlling relationship. You are their role model, what do you think this is imprinting upon them?

The Five love languages

The Five Love Languages is a book by Gary Chapman that one of my good friends introduced me to, and which I now recommend to every business owner and team member I work with. Feeling loved is a very important part of life. However, we all feel loved in different ways. We may hear someone say, 'They never loved me', but that may or may not be true, and we can't control whether or not others love us. However, whether we *feel* loved or not is not actually the other person's fault. According to Gary Chapman, we all have a different 'love language'. That means we all 'feel' loved in different ways. The five love languages are:

- Acts of service
- Words of affirmation
- Gifts
- Quality time
- Physical touch

Straight away, we can see why people may not feel loved if they have a love language that their loved ones don't use. So, for example, my top love language is 'words of affirmation'. When my husband and I were newly in our relationship, I liked him to tell me 'I love you' and hold my hand when we were walking down the street. However, his top love language is 'acts of service': he feels loved when I make him a cup of tea, not if I tell him I love him. So, there we were, speaking different love languages. I remember saying to him, 'You don't love me, you never tell me!' I would also get irritated when he would look at me and make a T sign with his fingers (indicating he would like me to make him a cup of tea). It was only after reading the book that we realised that me making him tea was one of his love languages (and it wasn't that he wanted me to do things for him all the time!). He, in turn, was able to start telling me he loved me rather than saying, 'You know I love you.' And when we walked down the street he would make an effort to hold my hand.

This sounds so simple but it was a revelation to me. It stopped me wasting energy and getting in a mood whilst walking along if he wasn't holding my hand. He'd just know to do it, or I would remind him and he'd say, 'Oh, yes, sorry.' Instead of having silly arguments or feeling unloved, we were able to ensure we felt loved by doing service via each other's love languages. Do we have the perfect relationship? Are we Barbie and Ken? Er ... no to both questions! However, it has definitely made us stronger and more understanding about what we need from each other. We also started using the five love languages in our relationship with family, and then with our team and clients. Again, it saved lots of energy, stopped miscommunication and allowed us to give 'bonuses' and rewards based on love languages. It saved us time and money, and made us better leaders. For example, there was no point in us spending money on a gift if the person's primary love language was quality time. A much better bonus would have been going for lunch and spending time together.

I remember once giving someone in my team a cash bonus for a great bit of work on a project. A few weeks later, that same person was complaining that they didn't feel appreciated. I was pretty upset as I'd only just given them a cash bonus a short while before. How could they now say they didn't feel appreciated? Gary Chapman's book includes a quiz you can take, so we asked the team to take it.

That's when we discovered that this lady's love language was 'words of affirmation'. In that moment, I realised I could have saved the cash and simply told her how marvellous she was, both one to one and in front of the team (although, in an ideal world, I'm sure she would have liked the cash *and* the words of recognition!). Take the quiz. Then get everyone you love to take the quiz. Then get your team to take the quiz! It will change how you view feeling loved, as well as how you show your love and appreciation to others. Another step towards becoming emotionally free.

Don't slag off others

I recently met up with someone who I had not seen for a while. During our conversation, this person started slagging off someone we both knew. Whilst they were bitching, I just nodded and listened, waiting for them to finish before changing the subject. They tried really hard to get me to join in, but I didn't. It is not that I am some sort of saint, it's just that as a Blue Cow womanpreneur, I don't get joy from slagging off others. And, anyway, logic has it that if the person is slagging someone else off to me, what might they be saying to others *about* me? So check in with yourself: how do you speak about others? You do not need to put others down or waste time moaning, you are here to light up the world. There is a saying: 'you do not have to blow out someone else's candles for yours to shine bright'. Be the Blue Cow beacon of light, not the brown cow bringer of darkness! I know life and business are not easy sometimes, however, whilst we cannot control *what* happens to us, we can control how we *respond* to what happens to us. I think Tony Robbins said that originally, and it really resonates with me.

Don't let others stop you living your dreams

A few years back, one of my good friends (the one who recommended *The Five Love Languages* to me – thanks, Avnish!) took me along to a Tony Robbins event called UPW. All I knew about this event was that we were going to 'unleash our power within', whatever the hell that meant. To be honest, I didn't like the sound of it one bit.

On arriving, I found myself in a room with 12,000 people who were (in my opinion) all crazy. They were dancing to the music, jumping on chairs, high fiving each other, hugging, and I was way out of my comfort zone. I remember saying to my friend, 'Well, it's been great, but I don't really think this is for me so I'm going to head off.' He persuaded me to stay and I only agreed as he was my friend. However, instead of joining in, I sat down on my chair, folded my arms, refused to high-five anyone who came near me and made it very clear that I would not be hugging strangers, unlike the rest of the delegates. In short, I began to act like a total brown cow.

When Tony came on stage, everyone cheered as if he were a superstar. He started teaching us, and I found myself taking notes. After a while, I took part in a few goal-setting exercises and even gave someone a high-five at the end. As the day progressed, I started to relax and actually enjoy what I was learning and, by lunchtime, I was really having fun. After lunch, they called 'dancers' onto the stage (as they'd done in the morning) and I watched as people volunteered to go up and motivate the crowd. By afternoon break, I had made the decision that, when they asked for the volunteer dancers again, I would go up to the front, get on stage and dance.

Now, let's put this into context. If you had ever seen my dancing skills, you would know there was absolutely no reason for me to imagine for one minute that I was a suitable candidate to be a dancer on stage, leading 12,000 people. My moves are rather challenged! But, when the time came, I made my way up there and said to the guy, 'Hi, I'm here to volunteer to dance on stage.' He looked at me and said, 'We have enough dancers, thanks.'

I was horrified. I had geared myself up, got myself 'in state' (one of the things Tony teaches us to do) – and now I was being told *no!* I returned to my seat, feeling defeated and deflated, and immediately started complaining – bitching and slagging off the guy who'd turned me away – and telling my friend how we should leave right now. I was really going for it, complaining big style, and waiting for him to agree with me so we could storm out in disgust.

However, instead of doing so, my friend looked at me and taught me an important lesson about the power of our peer group.

'Why are you complaining to me?' he asked. 'If you want to dance on the stage, go and make it happen. Dance on the stage, don't let anyone stop you.'

At that moment, I was even more angry. I couldn't believe it. In my head I was shouting, 'Call yourself a friend? You should be bitching with me and storming out!' Instead, he carried on dancing happily.

So, I had a decision to make. Should I leave? Should I sit down and cease joining in? Did I blame the person who'd said no? Did I stay pee-d off with my friend? Or, should I summon up the courage to go back to the stage?

I didn't have much time left because the dancing would stop soon so I made my decision – and made my way back to the stage. I said to the dance leader, 'I'm here to dance on stage,' with such certainty that he let me past. I then decided that it wasn't enough for me to be hidden at the back of the stage behind all the other dancers – I had an urge to dance at the front. I had no idea where this came from, bearing in mind I thought myself a terrible dancer and was always too embarrassed to dance at a party. However, there I was, at the front of the stage, in front of 12,000 people!

Yes, I must have looked ridiculous. I was completely out of time and probably appeared to be dancing to an entirely different song to the rest. Then it reached a point where not only was I fully immersed in my new status as a dancer, but it was as if I'd begun to imagine I was ... wait for it ... *Britney Spears!* Yes, from the video where she is dancing in the gold leotard. There I was up the front, shaking it about, wobbling my wobbly bits, arms all over the place, and in that moment I was free. For those couple of minutes, it was the first time in my life when I hadn't cared what anyone thought. I didn't care if I was good enough – if I looked fat, stupid, was in time, or if I was fitting in. In those glorious few minutes, I was fully free.

Just as Britney (me) was getting warmed up, the song ended and everyone started to leave the stage. I was elated. Rather than taking responsibility, I could have continued to blame others when things hadn't gone my way, moaning and bitching in a brown cow way. And I'd have probably given up. But I hadn't. And I returned to my seat extremely grateful to my friend.

What would you have done in this situation? What would your friends have done? This is a perfect example of how we cannot control what happens to us – but we can control how we respond to what happens to us. When we take this on board and act on it, we are another step forward to freeing ourselves emotionally.

It is also a reminder of the importance of having a Blue Cow peer group. Be sure to join our free Facebook group (Blue Cow Women in Business), as you will find an awesome Blue Cow community there. **www.facebook.com/groups/bluecowwomeninbusiness/**

Let's consider your business and life for a moment. What are you not doing because you've either been told 'no' or you are filled with doubt? Maybe you have been busily blaming others for your lack of being where you want to be?

'They made me feel like crap'

Another way to start the process of becoming emotionally free and changing your mindset is taking responsibility for how you feel.

We've all had times when we may have said, or we've heard others say, 'This person made me feel like crap.' What's very important is to have the realisation that we are the only ones who can control how we feel about what happens to us, how others behave towards us, and how we interpret that. People treat us how we allow ourselves to be treated.

I'd never thought of it this way before. I had to come to terms with the fact that I was the one in control of my emotions and how I felt around people and in certain situations. For years I'd been telling my story about how this person made me feel this and that person made me feel that. But it was all an illusion. I either had to take ownership of my feelings and not allow myself to believe that people made me feel that I was not enough, rubbish, fat, etc. – or I would have to remove those people from my life and not see them as much, if at all. Or I would have to do both of those things.

Consider yourself. Do you use this phrase: 'That person made me feel XYZ'? If so, I urge you to stop and look at yourself, take responsibility, and control how you feel, without thinking others make you feel anything. I quoted this earlier, however I love it so much, I am going to say it again: 'No one can make you feel inferior without your consent.' Eleanor Roosevelt.

My definition of success is:

Being able to do what I love, where I choose, with whom I choose, earning the money I deserve, making a positive difference, feeling great about myself and feeling happy.

I could not have achieved my definition of success had I not worked on myself: the person I was being in my business and life. Be sure that your definition of success includes you being happy, healthy and well, and take action to achieve it.

Womanpreneur

'Reset Moment'

- Self-care is how we look after ourselves.
- It involves how we treat ourselves, speak to ourselves, and how we allow ourselves to be treated.
- How is your self-care?
- Are there any immediate changes you need to make? What is stopping you?
- What will the outcome be in two year's time if you do not make the change?

PART TWO

Empowering business model

INTRODUCING THE W.O.W. BUSINESS

Now we have spent some time working on ourselves and realise that there is no point trying to create a great business if we:

1. Don't know what we want.
2. Are holding ourselves back emotionally or with poor self-care, and settling.

The fourth step in the R.E.S.E.T formula is to create an empowering business model. I am going to tell you the strategy we used to create our six and seven-figure lifestyle businesses. A successful business brings us joy, money, time and success on our terms. There's no point working hard in our business if we end up with no life or living unhappily in the 'wrong field' or 'wrong island'.

We describe two types of business model:

1. A sole business owner/guru model
2. A team-based model, where you employ team members

What is a W.O.W. business?

It's a successful, profitable business that can run *with or without* the owner. A W.O.W. business gives you the opportunity to have it all: freedom, money, choice – whilst making a positive difference to those using your product or service.

If you are a solopreneur (womanpreneur working on your own), we want your business to be W.O.W. – meaning you don't have to work all hours to achieve your goals. You work little and often and charge premium rates for a premium product or service. We would also create additional income streams in your business that do not rely completely on you to deliver them.

If your business is employing team members, we want to design it so that the business can run without you there all the time, without it requiring your energy and skills for the day-to-day running. You are not trapped by your business.

This is how you leverage your time, money and freedom. So you can live the life you love.

How did we create our W.O.W. businesses and how can you create yours?

Our secret lies in our 'Five V Technology', with its five sections that fit together like a wheel. When all five components are working well together, your business can run like a well-oiled machine and, if you wish, it can become a W.O.W. business. This allows you to decide exactly what you *want* to do in your business, as well as what you *don't*. It shifts you from someone who either has a hobby business that doesn't make any money, or a business where you do everything (wear all the hats and it relies on your energy), to a W.O.W. business that allows you to grow it successfully by design.

Imagine a playground roundabout. We want you to own the roundabout and give it the occasional push to keep it going around every day. We don't want you owning the roundabout and being the one who has to push it constantly, or else it will stop turning. You can achieve this with our Five V Technology. It works for any business.

What is the Five V Technology?

The five Vs are as follows:

VIBE: This is the feeling people get when they interact with your business. Your vibe should be unique and something people either love or hate. No vanilla, 'we want to please everyone' type businesses here. In the words of Steve Jobs, 'If you want to please everyone, don't be a leader, sell ice-cream'. Your vibe also talks of your culture and what you allow for yourself and your business. From a womanpreneur point of view, your vibe is how you show up! It's who you are in your business.

VELCRO: Velcro has two components. Firstly, it relates to the team you attract to work in your business – who you allow to represent you. So many people employ the wrong staff, which can lead to tons of issues, challenges and stress. We don't want you to have miserable staff acting like brown cows representing you in your business. We want you to have inspired Blue Cows.

Secondly, Velcro relates to your ideal customers, ensuring that you're attracting and keeping them. We don't want your business to be right for *everyone*. We want you to work with your ideal customers; customers who become raving fans, love to use your services, are happy to pay and refer people just like them.

VOYAGE: There are three voyages in your business:

- *The Owner Voyage*. What is the point of having a business if the owner is stressed out and unhappy? Your business should bring you joy, not stress! It's important to design a voyage that takes you to your dream 'field'.
- *The Customer Voyage.* This is the step-by-step experience your customer has from the minute they make contact with your business until the conclusion (although, hopefully, there won't be a conclusion and each customer will become a raving fan who repeatedly buys from your business).
- *The Team Member Voyage.* Your inspired Blue Cow team members need a compelling voyage so they know how they are doing, where they are going and how they can progress – and will keep loving being part of your team.

VISIBILITY: This is how your business becomes visible to your target customer. There is no point having a great business if your ideal customers don't know it exists. You should automate your visibility so that you have a regular and steady stream of new clients and customers.

VISCERAL: This is the final component that works like a repeat business model. You want clients and customers who choose to stay with you. It's much better to look after the customers you have, keep them and have repeat business than it is to purely focus on getting new customers. This is a huge mistake that many businesses make, and this V stops your business from 'emptying out' every month, leading to money worries and stress.

The Five V Technology might sound very simplistic but it is life-changing! When you implement these five Vs, along with the principles discussed in the first two chapters of this book, your business and your life will never be the same again. With this technology, you can create a six- or seven-figure business that gives you more money, more time, more freedom and less stress. Not only did it transform our business, it has now transformed the lives of Blue Cow client around the world. So let's dig deeper into how to put these 'Vs' into practice.

4
VIBE

'I've learned that people will forget what you said, people will forget what you did, but people will never forget how you made them feel.'

MAYA ANGELOU

The 'vibe' is a feeling. An emotion. It is felt by all those who work in your business and all those who visit or buy from it. It will *give* (or it should give if it's created properly) a feeling every time. It is made up of two important elements: intention and culture.

Intention

The intention of the business determines what your business looks and feels like. Every business needs an intention, and must be set by the owner. When we set the business intention with our clients, we clearly define what the business stands for and the outcomes they want from it. The intention gives focus and energy to the business. It will influence the decisions we make and the outcomes we achieve. It will dictate what is acceptable and what is not. As a womanpreneur, you must decide your intention for your business and then create it so it serves you.

You should regularly ask yourself the question:

Is what I'm doing right now taking me towards my business intention?

If the answer is no, then change what you're doing! Your actions should drive the business in line with the intention. If you're feeling stressed, burned out and full of worries and doubt, then your actions and business intention may not be congruent.

What type of womanpreneur do you want to show up as in your business? I used to believe that, in order to appear as a successful businesswoman and be taken seriously, I had to show up in a certain way, with a certain 'success vibe'. However, the vibe I'd created to 'look the part' was not actually authentically me. When I became more 'conscious' and aware, unleashing my inner womanpreneur vibe, I became much more authentic. For example, I love wearing jeans and sparkly trainers. Yet, in the past, when I went on stage,

I never believed I was 'allowed' to wear these. Until, one day, when I decided I *would* wear my smart jeans and sparkly trainers – and I instantly felt much more connected to who I wanted to be as a speaker and womanpreneur. Now my sparkly shoes have become part of my vibe and my brand.

I believe that appearance is an important aspect that helps set our vibe. So, however you show up as a professional woman, the smarter you look, then perhaps the more seriously you are taken. But you should also always turn up as you! I decided I would let my results dictate how seriously I am taken and, if I want to turn up in smart jeans, jacket and sparkly trainers, then I do. Another part of my vibe is that I always like to have my hair and nails looking nice. I feel so much better about myself (remember I am doing this for *me*!) when I have nicely painted nails on my hands and feet, and also when my hair is done. Having a regular hair wash and blow dry used to feel like a luxury, but not anymore. It's part of my vibe since I discovered the joy of having a blow dry without having to have a haircut first!

Think about your vibe and then create it consistently. Don't feel guilty – add it to your business budget. When we feel great about ourselves, our confidence grows and we show up in our business and life feeling more empowered. Make an effort to always show up as the best version of yourself, feeling as great about yourself as you can. Self-care and taking time to make the best of yourself is investing in yourself, and this should be a priority, not seen as a luxury.

My good friend, Mirela Sula (CEO of Global Woman), has a very professional vibe. She encourages all her members to show up dressed-up and smart. She always looks as though she's ready to attend a high-end event or wedding. She has her unique vibe, which is very inspiring. We love hanging out together, yet our vibe is different and that is okay. We are both successful 'Blue Cow' womenpreneurs. You are too, so be who you are! My vibe is a jean-wearing, sparkly-shoed, cheerful, happy and maybe 'over the top to some people' kinda gal. If anyone considers you 'too' happy, 'too' over the top and cheerful, *these are not your people*! Don't change your vibe to please others. Instead, crank it up (authentically) and you will attract and inspire those who are right for you.

In the words of Judy Garland, 'Always be a first-rate version of yourself and not a second-rate version of someone else.'

An amazing Womanpreneur client of mine, who runs a cleaning business, said she wanted her vibe to be smart, so she could show up to her home consultations in a suit or dress. The challenge was that, as she was just starting out in business, it was hard to afford multiple different outfits. I explained that I'd been there too and asked if she'd considered buying these items from charity shops and mixing and matching them. She looked at me in complete shock and said, 'Do successful women wear items from a charity shop?' – to which I replied, 'Yes, if money is tight at the moment and they want a selection of smart outfits!' Dressing smartly doesn't have to cost a fortune, so don't let that be an excuse! Just a note here: an old client of mine would regularly show up dressed in her PJs or running gear, without having had a shower, and get dressed at work. She would look messy, with that 'just got out of bed' look. This is perhaps fine 'backstage'. However, in front of customers who didn't know that she was not officially 'at work yet', or in front of team members who she'd be holding accountable for their wearing proper uniform, this wasn't giving a great vibe.

So, when I say be you and be authentic, whatever you decide your vibe to be, still ensure that the vibe your customers and team see is the one that represents who you are in business (and not the scruffy, vegged-out version reserved for pizza and PJ night). It might be authentic – I love vegging on the settee in my (Blue Cow) onesie and socks that have 'If you can read this, bring me wine' written on the soles, but I wouldn't turn up to a new client consultation wearing this outfit!

Designing your vibe is vital. Consider how your customers might feel when they interact with it – the vibe you give off and the vibe of your business. You also have to decide this latter element, the vibe of your business. What do you want people to *feel* when they interact with your business? Whatever it is, it should be what you intend them to feel and not left to chance.

Look

What is their first impression? Are they wowed by your look? Do you appear as a stressed-out struggling woman in business, or a professional, happy, confident-in-your-own skin womanpreneur?

If your business has a physical space, does your space look the same as every other mediocre business, with dull walls and boring chairs? Or have you created something special and unique? A space you love that represents your vibe?

Is your building well-maintained? Do you have dirty windows, rubbish lying on the ground? Broken signage or lights? Weeds growing by your front door? Do you have a branded car or van?

Are your indoor signs framed with your logo or stuck up with Blu-tack on scrappy-looking bits of paper? Do you have outdated, messy signs on overcrowded noticeboards? Do you have hundreds of leaflets lying everywhere?

Do you have a strong, consistent brand? Do you have a uniform that is maintained to a high standard so your team look world-class?

Are your team members smart? Is their hair tidy? Do they wear too much make-up? Are their shoes clean? Are they rushed? Are they too busy, too chatty, or miserable?

If you work virtually and have a more digital space, what vibe does that give off? Does it look the same as everyone else's or does your online vibe stand out?

Smell

What do customers smell when they enter your premises? Is it the smell of someone's lunch? Is it a specifically chosen aromatherapy oil?

Sound

What do your customers hear? We encourage everyone *not* to play the radio because you have no say in the vibe that is created by the songs chosen, the news read and the general banter and discussion. Choose a sound and genre of music that represents your vibe.

Feel

How do you want your clients and customers to feel? Are they sitting on plush chairs or hard benches? Do they feel welcome and part of the community?

Womanpreneur

'Reset Moment'

Intention is what you intend people to experience and how you intend to show up in your business. Consider yours. How do you show up? What is your 'work style' appearance? Do you feel guilty spending time and money on your appearance, yet appreciate that looking and feeling great will inspire others and yourself? If so, how can you reframe this?

Now consider your business intention. How do you want your customers to feel when they interact with your business?

Culture

The second part of *vibe* is your culture.

Culture is the *how we do things here*. The culture you create and allow to exist will determine whether you and your business are more Blue Cow or brown cow in their vibe. People behave towards you and treat you the way you allow them to. So be sure to create a culture with intention, rather than just allowing everyone else (team or clients) to dictate the culture.

Firstly, it's important to set the culture for yourself as the owner of your business. One of the challenges we face as womanpreneurs (and we've already touched on this) can be balancing family life with running our businesses. An awesome Blue Cow client of mine explained that she was at home with her two kids when her business manager called and started asking about his bonus. At the time, my client was busily trying to feed her kids, one of whom was being particularly disruptive and disagreeable. Any one of us who has kids knows exactly what this is like and appreciates that talking to their business manager about bonuses whilst little Jimmy is having a tantrum on the floor is far from ideal. My client reported that, as the conversation went on, 'Jimmy' was becoming more and more distressed, the business manager was growing more and more aggressive and my client was getting more and more angry, frustrated and emotional – and heading towards a meltdown herself.

When she finally got off the phone, having had to agree to a bonus she didn't want to give, she was feeling 'low' (which is putting it politely). My client was angry with the business manager and at her kids. Once we'd then talked it through, she saw how she'd allowed a culture to grow where her team could phone her at any time of day or night and she would feel compelled to either drop everything she was doing at home, or try to carry on being 'Mummy' at the same time as discussing business or sorting team issues. This was extremely disempowering to her. I have done this myself in the past and it never leads to an empowered womanpreneur. Hence why I wanted to ensure she changed this culture.

After our discussion, my client could see that she needed to create boundaries. We began by making a timetable that clearly set out when she was available to the business and team, and when she was not available, unless it was an absolute emergency. We defined an emergency as 'something only the business owner could deal with that had to be decided in that very moment and could not be answered in an email'. We agreed that never again would she answer her work phone, or a personal phone that came up with a work number, whilst she was feeding the kids, on a play date, bathing them, doing bedtime story or any other mummy or home task that needed her attention. Her kids and family deserve that attention, not the manager who showed no concern for the kids or the business owner during the stressed phone call.

If he had had some social acuity, he would have felt just how difficult this conversation was for the business owner at this time, and would have asked to book a more suitable moment to discuss his bonus. He could have waited and the owner *should* have created a culture where he did. He acted like a brown cow but, actually, so did the business owner! We have to empower ourselves, run our businesses and live our lives on our terms, not complain when we allow people to treat us in an unacceptable way.

I recently did a consultation call with a fabulous lady who had 'lost her way' in business and life. She explained that she had bought a business and, at first, it had been running well. But then she'd had staff challenges, money issues and the usual hurdles that womanpreneurs face. She said that she'd taken a day off to spend with her teenage daughter and, while they were out shopping, one of her employees had called her to 'ask what she was doing as she was not at work'. The business owner being checked up on by her team was a clear indication that she had not set boundaries or promoted a culture that empowered either her or her team. We laughed and agreed that 'None of your damn business!' wasn't a suitable response, but that setting new boundaries, intention and culture certainly was. Your business should give you the freedom to choose when you work and when you don't. You don't want to be worrying about your team or business when you're taking time off. As you grow your business, consider creating a leadership team who will take over the day-to-day running and help to move the business into growth without it relying on your being there every day.

Every Womanpreneur *must* develop strong intention and culture for her business, for the sake of it *and* her own sanity. It's key to stopping the challenge of trying to please everyone all at once and never feeling as though we're being successful in every area of our lives. Your ideal clients and team will respect this culture. It doesn't make you less successful or professional. It makes your vibe much more Blue Cow, as it demonstrates that you respect yourself enough to take time off and your family enough to give them your attention. Value yourself and your loved ones by setting boundaries in your business. Having a strong intention and culture means that when you are not there in your business, it will still run positively in the way you have intended it to run.

Womanpreneur

'Reset Moment'

Consider your timetable. When are you available to your team? To your customers? When are you not available? Being available 24 hours a day is not necessary; it is unhealthy, no matter how much we love our business.

Blue Cow culture in your team

So, whether you have one team member or twenty, you must develop your culture. 'Culture' is defined in the *Oxford English Dictionary* as 'the total of the inherited ideas, beliefs, values, and knowledge, which constitute the shared bases of social action'. Your culture is the very thing that sets you apart from other businesses like yours. It forms the basis of the 'this is how we behave here; this is who we are, and these are our standards'. A clear culture will attract like-minded people to your business and repel those who should not be a part of it. When people walk into your business – whether clients or potential team members – they should feel the culture and know immediately whether they love or hate it.

The culture of your business comes from your intention. It is the predetermined, 'this is how we do things here' ethos. A consulting client of ours recently told us (after a discussion about culture): 'Looking at my current team, it's clear I need to change them all. None of them subscribe to our culture: they all do what suits them and refuse to follow the intention I have for my business.' Our client complained about having to give energy to staff working in her business who didn't want to work to her rules. She'd found herself with people acting like brown cow complainers, who moaned about how hard they had to work and how busy they were. They called in sick a lot, took endless breaks and showed up late. This was their culture and it certainly wasn't going to take the business very far.

The business owner had had enough, so I helped her create a culture that reflected her deepest wants and desires – a positive place where Blue Cow team members were happy and energised and followed her rules. We discussed the fact that her current team (who were acting like brown cows) might want to leave once this was in place, and I asked if she was prepared to deal with that. She replied that things had to change and she knew they wouldn't if she didn't take action.

As a result of changing the culture, my client kept just one member of her original team. All the others left in the months that followed. While it was a difficult time for her, some of the departing staff were not very pleasant about her or the business changes, which just showed how the business owner did the right thing by not having those people representing her any more. The one remaining person was transformed by what had happened and became the leader of a great new Blue Cow team. This person helped recruit a fresh team full of Blue Cows who were clear from the start that 'this is how we do things here', and happy to be part of that culture.

The great thing about this process is that when you uphold your new Blue Cow culture, as a womanpreneur, you don't have to 'sack' anyone. In this case, when the complainers realised my client meant business, they left. There was nothing to keep them there once they decided the new culture wasn't one to which they wanted to subscribe.

One important point to note – please always get legal advice if you've employed team members whom you think may leave during the culture-cranking process, as this will affect how they depart. It takes courage to 'stick to your guns' as my client demonstrated. She had to overcome a great deal of negativity and handle angry staff members who didn't want things to change. Ask yourself if you would have the courage to do what she did.

Another amazing womanpreneur I work with owns a café. I recently went there, prior to a meeting, to do some work. There was a young girl working there as a waitress, and when I tried to get her attention, to order a tea and a bit of cake, she kept ignoring me. After repeated attempts, I ended up waving rather wildly at her as she walked past, until, finally, she came over. When I asked her if I could order a drink, she looked at me without any hint of a smile, said 'yes'. As she walked away, she looked extremely fed up. So much so, that I felt bad for having asked her!

Now, imagine you're the business owner. What vibe is that team member creating? What is the culture like that *allows* a team member to act in that way towards customers? How much more business could they be doing if, instead of looking miserable and fed up, that waitress had been smiling, happy and looking out for customers with empty cups that needed refilling – in other words, helping them spend money in the business?

So, will the womanpreneur owner move this lady on and replace her with a Blue Cow version? Or will she settle and let her continue to set the wrong vibe and culture? If the owner does allow this to carry on, it won't take long for the other Blue Cow team members to either leave, or for the whole team to turn into miserable, brown cow people. The owner will then wonder why the business isn't making as much money as she knows it could.

You have the right to employ, lead and work alongside passionate Blue Cow team members who want to do the best job they can and are motivated to help your business be great. Your team deserves to work with a strong, inspiring Blue Cow leader, who has high standards for herself and her business, in line with the business intention. With a strong, positive culture, the 'thank goodness it's Friday' negative people won't want to join you, and if they do accidentally get in, they won't hang around long. Don't give your energy to negative people (and having to waste time trying to energise them or dealing with the issues they create). Your culture will encourage them to leave – no more messing you about, calling in sick or moaning and bitching – and you can let them go with love to become some other business owner's nightmare! Hopefully, Blue Cows who are in the wrong field will also be empowered to leave and find a business like yours that inspires them.

This aspect is common in many businesses with whom I consult. I'll find a frustrated owner 'putting up' with or being terrorised by staff.

When a business is started, it rarely has a strong culture in place. As time goes on, it will become a mishmash of individual wants and needs. The team members are invariably led by the person in the group with the strongest character. This is not necessarily the owner, official leader or manager, and when it isn't, the other person's needs are almost never in line with the business owner's needs and vision for the company. Ultimately, this leads to stress all round, for the business owner and for the team, and stress 'backstage' will always eventually start to affect the customer experience.

Staff resistance to raising the bar and creating a Blue Cow culture can be high. It's a bit like our kids having always been allowed to stay up past their bedtime at 8pm. They know their bedtime is 8pm but no one upholds this, least of all the shattered, worn-out mum, who doesn't have the energy to argue. When one day the mum does decide to uphold bedtime or, even worse, make it earlier, the kids get angry and rebellious, feeling their rights are being taken away. Yet, in fact, this situation has only come about due to either unclear guidelines or a lack of upholding those guidelines. If the mum wants bedtime back at 8pm, she's going to have to be prepared to lead, to not be liked and to not give in. It's the same in our businesses.

Creating your Blue Cow culture

We've already established that the culture of a business is derived from the intention and can be thought of as 'this is how we do things here'. The culture consists of a mixture of other things too: the standards, the business recipes and the community of team players. In all my businesses, I've found it invaluable to use a metaphor for the culture. The most powerful cultural metaphor you can use is Blue Cow. Everyone in my businesses knows what it means and loves my business culture being defined by that name. The Blue Cow is enthusiastic, optimistic, open-minded, passionate, has high energy and is open and honest.

During job interviews I conduct, and now those conducted by my consultancy clients, I talk to interviewees about Blue Cow and tell them that, in order to 'play in our team', they have to want to play their best; not *be* the best, necessarily, but to *want* to be *their* best. There is a difference. I'm not necessarily looking for 'superstars' to work in my business; I'm looking for a 'superstar' attitude.

I was recently talking to a new manager, in one of the businesses with which I consult, about a team member who 'refused' to follow their business tenets. This included shaking a client's hand on arrival, covering other team members' annual leave, and learning the business recipes. The 'non-subscriber' was well-liked, and the manager was concerned about upsetting the team if she rocked the boat by calling this employee out for not subscribing to the company culture. I explained that this wasn't personal and that the manager needed to take action, or the culture would become further diluted by this person, resulting in unhappy Blue Cow team members who *were* subscribing to the culture.

A world-class Blue Cow culture is not a hostage crisis; it should attract Blue Cow team players who want to play full out in your team. Anyone who doesn't want to uphold and follow the tenets should be encouraged positively to choose a different team.

What would you do in this situation? Be courageous and 'rock the boat' or settle and allow standards to drop? I've met clients who do both. The ones who make the change, standing up for themselves and the way they want things done, see tremendous rewards. Those who back down, settle, and give in to a brown cow culture are just heading for more burnout and frustration. Only this week I read a post in a business forum by a business owner who told how some of her staff were bitchy and complaining. As a result, two of her best team members had left, leaving her with just the bitchy, complaining ones. She was asking in the forum what she should do. This is very common! Blue Cows don't want to hang around in a team that has a brown cow culture and, even more, they don't want to work with a boss who's not prepared to lead, take control and eradicate the brown cow behaviour. So the Blues leave, leaving the uninspired people who are working in the wrong field. The womanpreneur may not realise what's going on and can find herself stuck in a recruiting circle where she attracts great people, who start working in the business – and then leave. Until the brown cow culture is changed, you will not keep Blue Cows in your team.

I recently went on a 'mummy and daughter' dinner date with our six-year-old. We found ourselves sitting right next to another table, so close that it was as if we were all having dinner together. For the entire duration of our meal, the two ladies next to us discussed work. Well, to be honest, one lady talked about her work whilst the other listened. The talking lady was clearly unhappy and told her friend at great length all the things she was unhappy about, all the people she didn't like, as well as various pieces of 'office gossip'. It went on and on. I was praying my daughter wouldn't want dessert so I wouldn't have to hear any more. Alas, you guessed it, of course my daughter wanted dessert! Whilst she munched on the chocolate fudge cake, the lady continued. We had to hear all about how 'Doris had to be moved upstairs because we couldn't get on' and how she wasn't speaking to this person because of X Y Z.

Oh, my word! I had to stop myself interrupting and asking her: 'If you're that unhappy, why haven't you left?' I didn't because we weren't officially having dinner together. However, was it her fault? Surely the more appropriate question was: why was she still allowed to be part of that team? Perhaps the owner or manager was really more at fault, for allowing her to stay in that business and team, acting and feeling this way. The negative brown cow culture must have been bringing everyone down. This lady certainly had nothing positive to say. And you can bet that if the manager or owner did try to create a positive Blue Cow culture, this lady wouldn't be pleased and would cause all manner of trouble. I'm sure she was a nice person but she was clearly working in the wrong 'field'. The longer we keep these people in our team, the more stress we will have – and the less energy we can give to the Blue Cows and the work we need to put in to create the intention of the business and drive it forward.

Strategies for a Blue Cow culture

It should be remembered that creating a Blue Cow culture and maintaining it is a team effort, led by the leaders. Below is a selection of tools I use to build and maintain the Blue Cow culture:

A service agreement or contract

Every team member should read and sign a copy of their contract or service agreement. This sets out the 'terms' under which they can join and stay in the team.

A clear job description

This is the role you want that team member to play in your business. It avoids confusion and conflict, as everyone is clear what they are expected to do as part of the team. It also helps your Blue Cows be successful as they have clarity and certainty.

The team Blue Cow courtesy system

This is a system to ensure that team members respect and care about each other, as well as your clients. Come together as a team and create a list of acceptable Blue Cow and unacceptable brown cow behaviours in your team.

A weekly coaching session

Every star sports player has a coach to help them reach their potential. You should have a coach and your team needs your coaching. I advocate holding weekly coaching sessions for all team members on subjects that range from outstanding customer care, through to communication, sales and personal growth.

The monthly meet

It should be 'compulsory' for every team member to attend (the word 'compulsory' isn't normally necessary for Velcro Blue Cow team members). Whether they are full-time or part-time, I make it a condition for staying in my field. Sometimes clients tell us their team members 'try to make the coaching sessions and monthly meet when they can', but we always encourage them to rethink this. World-class teams train together. You would never see a world-class football team winning the World Cup with players who 'made the training sessions when they could'.

In my business, we vote for a Blue Cow Team Member of the Month, and that person wins £30 in vouchers. I also give updates and feedback on areas the team need to know about.

The huddle

At the start and end of every shift, have a team huddle. The purpose of this is to reaffirm what you want to achieve as a team, set the intention for the shift and check in with everyone. At the end of the day, get each member of the team to feed back two positive things and one not-so-positive thing that happened during the shift, then immediately suggest ways they could improve on the next. In this way, everyone starts and ends their working day feeling great. This should be a 'power session'.

A birthday system

Celebrate each team member's birthday with a joint gift and card from everyone. Ask every person to contribute £1 for each team member in the business on a yearly basis – so if there are 30 team members, then each contributes £30 per annum. Celebrating birthdays helps boost team morale and, if your team members feel great about themselves and each other, they will also feel great about looking after your clients. Blue Cows love to celebrate others' special days and achievements, especially those of their Blue Cow teammates.

Blue Cow strategy days

Four times a year, we close our business for two days so all the team can attend our strategy days. The first day and a half we spend working on ourselves and on the business (on *our* growth and expansion; on *its* growth and expansion), as well as on our skills and goals for the business. For the second half of day two, we go off and take part in a team-building activity. Over the years, we've done all sorts of things: from spa days to army assault courses; zookeeper days to fire-walking over hot coals; board-breaking to overcome limiting beliefs to climbing high ropes and playing the 'Apprentice' game. We have shot rifles, run, crawled and climbed (blindfolded!), and relaxed and laughed and cried. All as a team. This activity component of strategy days is always high energy and action-packed. We often see huge team breakthroughs, as team morale and support are paramount. These days should not be 'boring classroom sessions'; they should be inspiring, educational and help your team with professional and personal mastery. We have run hundreds of strategy days for our own teams and those of our clients and, every time, these days work amazingly to help bond a team, inspire them and rally them to the business cause.

The holiday/absence system

When a team member cannot be present at the business due to annual leave or unexpected absence, it is their responsibility to find another team member to cover for them. The goal is that 'the show must go on', and I suggest you take that very seriously. Create clear, strong systems that allow your Blue Cow business to 'go on' when key players are on holiday. Please kindly note that Blue Cows are reliable; they don't have lots of time off due to sickness. If you're shutting elements of the business or telling customers you're 'short-staffed' because someone is on annual leave, we encourage you to change this as it can massively affect your business capacity and finances. You will still have the same overheads but less income.

Maintaining the Blue Cow culture

As we said earlier, while it's your job to ensure all team members are playing on the right team, it's up to the team to maintain the standards and intention. When someone falls short, any team member can support them and help them back to being the best they can be. Equally, if someone is not playing the game and is creating issues or challenges, the team can nudge them gently to get them back on track. Not allowing mediocrity into the team is a team effort.

A strong, loving Blue Cow culture creates an empowering environment – a supportive, encouraging setting for all those who subscribe to it. If you get it right, be prepared for other people – those outside your business – to call your business a 'cult'. That is exactly the reaction you are after! It *is* a 'cult' after all — a '*cult*-ure'! You know you are doing something great if your culture gets described that way. A cult of positive people who want to be the best they can be. How amazing!

Womanpreneur

'Reset Moment'

- Do you have an intention for your business? If you do, write it down
- If you don't, then write some keywords to get you started
- Are there things you would like to change about your vibe?
- Are there things you would like to change about your culture?
- If you were very brave, what would you change?

In summary:

- To achieve your dream business, you must have a strong, clear intention and culture
- Your Blue Cow culture should exist with or without you being physically present in your business
- Vibe is engendered in your clients through their five senses. Deliberately create yours – don't let it just develop
- As a Blue Cow leader, you need to ensure you create a culture that serves you and allows you to segment your business time and family life
- Do not allow team or customers to encroach on family time
- Show up on your terms looking professional and smart – your way

5
VELCRO

'When you speak to everyone, you speak to no one.'

MEREDITH HILL

'Velcro' relates to our team and our ideal customers.

Let's talk about team first.

'How do I attract really good people to work in my business?' That's a question I hear all the time. The womanpreneur asking it will usually follow it up with: 'And how do I keep them?'

This is where the 'stickability' of your business comes in: its ability to act like Velcro to current and potential team members. After all, this is what most businesses want: a happy team of motivated Blue Cows pushing the project forward, rather than a group of unmotivated staff who are not that bothered one way or another and who act like brown cows.

The first thing to remember is the difference between 'staff' and 'team'. In the UK, staff are the individuals you pay to come and be physically present in your business. They carry out a job that they are paid to do. Your Blue Cow team, on the other hand, is a group of team members who work together to achieve a common goal in line with the intention of your business. There is an oft-repeated acronym that might sound a bit corny these days but is true nonetheless:

Team:
Together Everyone Achieves More

So banish the word 'staff' from your vocabulary and your Blue Cow business right now! Your team members are your Blue Cow herd. They are the people you put together to represent you and your business, so be sure that these people are worthy of representing you.

Attitude

The number one thing you're looking for from a great team member is a great attitude. You can teach dress code, business systems and all the rest of it but you can never teach someone to have a great attitude. In my husband's and my businesses, we would much rather have an inexperienced, fresh person with a great attitude than someone who is experienced with a bad attitude. One of the best team members we had, started out with us as a work experience kid. However, she stayed on afterwards and became one of our 'Saturday team'. If you asked her to do anything, she always replied, 'Of course I can.' She was eager, cheerful and one of the brightest, most diligent team members we had ever had the pleasure of employing – yet she was less than 18 years old. She was a Blue Cow from the very start. You deserve 'of course I can' team members.

The Blue Cow captain Vs the brown cow bad boss

The Blue Cow attitude is set by the captain and then followed and upheld by the team. In my vocabulary, the boss and the captain are two different animals. Before you start recruiting your team, you need to work on being a Blue Cow captain. The captain is the leader, ultimately responsible for the business being a success. The team works alongside the captain to achieve a united outcome – reaching the goals initially set by the captain. A bad brown cow boss, on the other hand, tends to attract staff. Remember, staff are a group of individuals paid to do a job by the boss. They have no real vested interest in the project or its outcome. They do their job, put in their contracted hours and get paid for doing so. Then they go home.

I was once asked to give some coaching to a team member from a reasonably successful healthcare business. The business owner told us that the lady was very keen at the start and now seemed to have lost her 'mojo'. The owner wanted to discover what had gone wrong. Was she a bad hire or had she got lost along the way?

I sat with the team member and asked her to tell me about her role. She lit up and went into a lengthy explanation of how much she loved caring for the clients and educating them. She also loved being part of the business. But when I asked her about her captain (boss), her persona completely changed. She started to cry and explained how the business owner came in every day and didn't even say 'good morning'. She described how he walked past her and straight into his treatment room. She felt unworthy and isolated. She said the boss was always looking for the things she hadn't done correctly and never mentioned all the good things she'd done, so she felt criticised and undervalued.

To add to the frustration, the boss's spouse would call numerous times throughout the day to speak to the boss and, when he got off the phone, he was even more grumpy and off key. She expressed how difficult it was to be happy and polite and upbeat while the boss wasn't. And she cried even louder when she told me, 'He doesn't even know my name – he calls me Lynda but my name is Lydia. I haven't said anything because it's been going on for months.'

This is an example of 'bad boss' behaviour rather than 'great captain' behaviour. If we treat people as *staff*, they act like *staff*. Your team is a reflection of you. If you're going to lead a great team, you need to become a great captain. A team cannot flourish unless the team captain is determined to become a great leader. The most common reason why people leave a business is because of their boss or manager: a bad boss can never attract and retain great people.

Blue Cow behaviour Vs brown cow behaviour

I've already talked about Blue Cow and brown cow behaviour that womanpreneurs may display, so let's talk about the same thing for team members.

Remember the 'Saturday girl' who'd say, 'Of course I can!' every time she was asked to do something? Well, she was a Blue Cow from the get-go. We didn't have to persuade her, cajole her or reason with her to be a Blue Cow. She just *was* one. Not because of her experience or her knowledge; not because she understood our computer system or knew our clients by name, or any of the other skills you might assume marked her out as a Blue Cow. In fact, just the opposite was true. At the start, she knew none of those things. But with her attitude, great coaching and clear direction, how long do you think it took her to acquire those skills?

Ask your team: 'What sort of cow are you?'

This is something you should discuss with your team right from the beginning. Do they light up a room, for instance? Are they positive, inspiring and passionate? Or do they tend to be low energy or lethargic in your project but the opposite outside? Of course your business needs a mix of personalities, however everyone should bring positive energy to work. Ensure you tell your team (and prospective team members) the Blue Cow story. It gives them a perfect, easily understandable metaphor for the behaviour and the attitude you want in your business. Blue Cow team members don't tell us, 'Everybody knows we can't do that' or 'Everybody knows that won't work here' when we suggest new ideas and goals. They are optimistic and positive – even if a little scared.

By the way, as you read this, you're probably thinking of one or two (or even more) people who act like brown cows in your business, but masquerade as team members. You know the ones I mean: they'll be awkward, will resist change, will go off sick on a sunny day, stifle the growth of the business if they can, heckle or disagree with you – and they'll often be powerful within the group of employees. Please note I am not saying that anyone who is not an extrovert is acting like a brown cow. You will know the ones acting like brown cows as they are not in flow with the business. They tend to make tight friendships with other 'staff' members who are, like them, less than blue whilst in your environment. You know them by their lack of positive attitude, commitment and, ultimately, by the level of stress they bring you!

We must always remember, people aren't born Blue Cows or brown cows, but everyone has the ability to act like a Blue Cow or a brown cow. It's a daily choice we make.

I remember meeting a receptionist on a business visit who told me she couldn't answer the phone or check the answerphone messages as that would mean she would have to stop reading her novel. Certainly not Blue Cow behaviour! I've even experienced two receptionists having a full-blown argument in front of clients, ending with one shouting at the other that she was a 'patronising, f***ing b**ch'! These examples may sound extreme. However, I have seen countless other examples of brown cow behaviour: the receptionist who refused to take her winter coat and hat off, as she was cold in reception; those who wouldn't wear the correct uniform; someone who would eat their lunch sitting at the reception desk while customers were coming in, despite being asked not to; a team member talking on their mobile phone when supposed to be serving clients; someone refusing to greet customers with a smile, as they would be 'acting inauthentically'; a team member who talked to every customer about the awful divorce she was going through and cried frequently with them; and a business manager who asked a dental customer who was booking a course of treatment, 'Are you made of money?'

You name it and I've probably seen it.

All these people were not acting like Blue Cow team members and were clearly not working in the right field for them. However, it wasn't their fault. Business owners must take responsibility for the behaviours and standards that are allowed in their business. Full stop! If you are spending time blaming others, *stop it*. You have to be in charge in your business. People behave how you allow them to behave.

When you're striving for a Blue Cow team with amazing customer care, look out for any brown cow behaviour. This may include:

- Yawning in public
- Moaning and being negative
- Being late
- Looking scruffy
- Taking personal phone calls
- Texting their friends during a shift
- Organising their social life
- Ignoring customers

Decide what constitutes Blue Cow behaviour and brown cow behaviour in your team and make it clear the standards you expect.

The secrets of being a Blue Cow captain

It all starts with the womanpreneur deciding to be a Blue Cow captain and refusing to settle for a brown cow team. If you want to become a Blue Cow captain, there are a few basic principles to follow:

Set your standards

Decide on appearance, attitude, roles. If you don't have high standards, you won't build a team that has them.

Develop a positive outlook and lead from the front

Every business has its challenges, highs and lows. Your team need their captain to lead them positively in the good and not-so-good times.

Have high standards for yourself and your team

Blue Cows have high standards for themselves and their team. Never be late. Always look smart, clean and smell fresh, with polished shoes and an ironed shirt. Appearance and attitude are very important.

Numerous times I've consulted with business owners who say they want a world-class business yet they have dirty shoes, smell of body odour, run late, cancel meetings and don't set high enough standards for their business and team. You cannot achieve great things in your business with mediocre standards.

Choose your Blue Cow team wisely

Every member of your team represents you. I'm sure you've heard the saying, 'Hire slow, fire fast'. A brown cow isn't doing you a favour by being on your team. Use a DISC profile system that ensures the person you appoint has the correct skill set for the job. If you're looking for someone to work in the back office, they don't necessarily need great people skills but they do need great attention to detail. If you want an awesome customer service advisor, choose someone who loves people and wants to give awesome customer care.

Be respectful

To gain respect, give respect. Simple! I've already mentioned having a courtesy system and I recommend that all businesses implement at least this. Shouting at your team, no matter what they've done, is never the best way to empower them or encourage them to be better. It just makes you look like a brown cow! Giving respect garners respect. If you need to have a chat with a team member, always do it backstage. Never reprimand someone in front of others.

I hate the word 'reprimand': if you have to reprimand someone for not doing something they should have done, always consider whether you coached them well enough in the beginning. If you do need to 'correct behaviour', tell them clearly and non-emotionally, reset the standard, give them the chance to shine and provide positive feedback afterwards. This motivates a Blue Cow team. Telling them off and not allowing them to shine just makes them resentful and you frustrated. Blue Cows will leave and brown cows will moan.

Banish a negative mindset – 'They will find me out'

Many business owners live in fear that their team will 'find them out'. They worry the team will discover they are not the guru who has all the answers, and this can stop them from recruiting and leading great people. Instead, they look for people who are not as good as they are or are like themselves, rather than focusing on recruiting people who have different skills to their own and unleashing them into the business to do great things. Celebrate yourself for the Blue Cow you are; don't worry about the things you are not.

Get a Blue Cow coach or mentor

All serious athletes, professional sports players and great business owners do not expect to get to the top of their game alone. They all have at least one world-class coach or mentor alongside them, guiding them, extracting the best from them. All great womanpreneurs must follow this strategy. The mentor's job is not to tell the owner what to do but to help them stay focused on the business intention and assist with a strategy to keep them on course. They are a bit like a satnav: you tell them your destination and they help find the best way to get you there.

A business mentor is someone who has already achieved your goal – there is no need to reinvent the wheel. Get one! Speak to me and my team. We would love to support and mentor you.

Blue Cow captain Vs brown cow bad boss behaviour

When growing yourself as a leader, consider the following attitudes and habits of the brown cow bad boss:

- Not greeting team members by name
- Being grumpy
- Having different standards
- Reprimanding in public
- Abdication of responsibilities
- Allowing bullying
- Allowing poor team standards
- Allowing brown cow behaviour
- Breaking promises
- Cancelling meetings at short notice
- Not being smart and well-groomed (*no* BO/bad breath)

Blue Cow captain behaviour:

- Greeting team members with a smile
- Being respectful
- Being fair
- Being assertive
- Being a strong leader
- Smelling nice and looking smart
- Empowering your team
- Being a good decision-maker
- Communicating well
- Having fun
- Inspiring your team
- Wanting the best for team members
- Coaching the team.

When to recruit team members

A womanpreneur should recognise when it's a great time to recruit:

- You're energised to connect with a new team member and help them learn
- Your systems are working and you have time to support, coach and nurture the new team member
- Your business is about to go through a growth cycle.

Do NOT add team members when:

- You need a day off
- You feel burned out
- Your business is losing money, you want help to make it more successful, and you think they have the answers you need

The act of recruiting a new team member means you are prepared to invest time, energy and money in supporting and coaching them. Here is a warning, though. The type of thing I often hear is: *'the new person is going to be great. They seem very capable, which means I can leave them to it and take time off.'* No, you can't!

The new team member will require coaching (in your culture and strategies), and a mountain of positive input – technically and emotionally. And you will spend a not inconsiderable amount of money and time on the process. A new team member may waste or 'mismanage' many new clients during the initial period, as they will have no idea how to be successful in your business. Do not take this lightly.

Recruitment success

Recruitment is a large part of business success. I am asked time and time again the best way to recruit, and my strategy is fantastic for saving time and energy and attracting the right people. Let me share my recipe for recruiting receptionists. It will save you so much time and heartache.

I follow the acronym ATOAR, which stands for Advert, Talk, Observe, Away and Return.

A – Advert

The advertisement – whether in traditional places like local papers and noticeboards or on modern platforms such as social media or online job sites – has to stand out and be noticed. It has to be emotive in some way: funny, quirky or profound. Don't mention specific hours or salary.

T – Talk

Those who respond to the advert are invited to your business for a group session to hear more about the business and the role. Here is the wording my husband and I have used in our businesses:

Thank you so much for your interest in our position. We would like to invite you to a short group talk, where we will share all the information you need about the role and our company. Then, if you are keen to apply, we will meet with you one-to-one so you have the opportunity to ask any questions and then we will go from there. We have used this process successfully for many years and find it brilliant so that we do not waste your time if we are not the right place for you. Please do let us know if you will be attending.

You can either schedule the talk for a lunchtime or an evening. Do what suits you if you are the one leading the talk.

According to the numbers of responders, set up enough chairs to accommodate them. With a simple sign-in sheet, take note of the time each candidate arrives and use it as the order to speak to them one-to-one. This is also great to have because anyone who is late and does not apologise profusely is probably not going to be a Blue Cow team member!

I don't start poring over CVs at this stage. I also don't meet applicants at different times for one-to-one, 30-minute, life-force-draining interviews. If someone can't attend at the specified time, say you will invite them to the next group talk, as your business is growing and you will be adding more team members (which is true). If people call with questions, remember that you don't have time to answer, and simply say, 'We'll tell you everything at the group session.'

Invite everyone! The more, the merrier, as it gives great social proof that there is lots of interest in the role and your company. Also, bear in mind that lots of applicants will not show up.

Preparation for the session should include the following:

- Have sign-in sheets prepared (as mentioned) so you can track what time each person arrives
- Get the room ready
- Ensure your presentation technology works
- Start on time! Don't wait for latecomers
- Ensure you look really smart or are wearing your branded uniform
- Have your talk well-planned – it should last 20–30 minutes. This may seem daunting at first but you'll get used to it.

Your talk should include:

- Who you are
- A brief business history. Tell it as a story, not boring dates and facts
- A description of the role you're recruiting for and what that person will do
- The hours – for example, will it include shifts?
- The wages or salary
- The holiday allowance and how this works
- Your Blue Cow culture

The idea is that you 'scare off' people who are unlikely to be Velcro to your culture and inspire those who maybe want to know more. So tell them this role is not right for them if they are looking to work on their own and not as part of a team, only wanting to work weekdays or don't want to wear the uniform (delete as appropriate).

At the end, invite people to leave if this isn't the right role for them. This will save you wasting your time taking forward candidates who are not a good fit, as they'll know it's not what they're looking for.

Use the sign-in sheet as you meet with each candidate individually for five minutes in the order that they arrived. This is a screening process. You are looking for anyone who is not right for your business, who is not able to work the hours or wants different pay, etc. Don't try to fit a round peg into a square hole.

Ask them questions like:

- If you could do any job in the world, what would it be?
- £xx is the rate of pay here. How do you feel about that?
- Are you able to work the shift patterns/hours?

If you like them, offer them an opportunity to come and observe the role for an hour (you might offer this to one, two or a dozen, depending on how many responded to your advert and how many you like). The idea is that they see what they will be doing if they get the job.

O – Observe

Next, the prospective team member comes into your business for an hour and shadows a team member doing a similar job to the one on offer. If they are your first employee, they will be observing you in the role they will be taking over. Make sure the team member you choose is an 'über' culture subscriber. Unlike traditional interviews, never simply meet the candidate. Being with someone for a whole hour will allow you to see their energy, their initiative and how they interact with your clients and other team members. During the hour, ensure you talk about your intention and culture and, of course, your story. You want to avoid any surprises on day one, such as, 'I didn't know I'd have to wear a uniform', etc.

A – Away

Send them away and ask them to write an email to you with their feedback on how they found their time with your business: what they enjoyed and what they felt about the vibe and the culture. If they would like to apply, tell them to convince you in the email 'why I'd be mad not to add them to my team'.

R – Return

When they return, ask them again why they wanted to come back, and talk to them more about your business intention and the type of role you're offering. Describe the coaching you offer and any progression for them within your business. This is decision time! By now, you should have a good idea whether this person will be a good fit or not and whether or not they are likely to be a culture subscriber. You can go into detail around pay, benefits, contracts and so on, and offer them a probationary period of employment. If your culture is strong, you will know within a few weeks (often a few days) if this person is truly a good fit. Some womenpreneurs tell me they always give a six week probation, this is fine, however if you know someone isn't right, set them free as soon as you can. Please do not try to 'rescue' them or make them fit. If they are not suitable, call the next person on the list of those candidates who made a good impression on you and start the process again.

Recruiting this way (for 'general' team members) saves hours and hours of frustration. Before this, I'd spent time meeting with each person for standard, half-hour interviews. It took most of the day to see just a handful of people, most of whom I could tell were obviously not a good fit from the first few minutes of talking to them! The ATOAR method streamlines the recruitment process and gives you flexibility.

Never settle! If you need to repeat the process a few times, then do! Hire a temp in the meantime and keep energy high. You can't attract Blue Cows if you have low energy and a short-staffed vibe. Just a note here, a womanpreneur friend of mine, told me about a time where she hired a temp and then offered the temp the position in her business because she was too lazy to go through the recruitment process. She ended up regretting this decision for three years. This is a great reminder to us all, recruitment should be taken seriously as taking on the wrong person can cost you lots in wasted money, time and also increased stress.

You deserve Blue Cow team members who are passionate about your business and want to strive to be the best they can be. Anyone who doesn't want this is very welcome to go and join another project. Never worry about not being able to find someone to replace a team member. The nature of a highly dynamic environment means there is always someone who wants to step up. Create the hole and the universe will fill it every time. Your business is growing and you are always needing to recruit great people, so create a stress-free way of doing so.

But take care: there can be the temptation to 'rescue' people during the interview process. This means you might offer someone a job you know in your gut won't be suitable, because you feel sorry for them. Or you might take on the wrong candidate because you are desperate for someone to fill a gap in the team. If you think you may be about to make this mistake, review the following potential Blue Cow and brown cow behaviours and look out for them during the recruitment process:

Your ideal Blue Cows:

- Are on time
- Look smart
- Have clean shoes
- Don't have chipped nail polish that is at the end of its life and needs to be removed
- Look interested
- Live a reasonable distance from where they will be working
- Are happy with the pay scale and hours on offer
- Are interested in the product or service you sell
- Show up when they say they will during the recruitment process
- Have great energy
- Demonstrate good spelling and grammar in emails

Your potential brown cows:

- Are late
- Don't apologise for their lateness
- Yawn
- Look scruffy
- Look bored
- Don't show up
- Don't ask any questions
- Say they're happy with part-time but ideally want full-time (or vice versa)
- Want more pay than you're offering
- Don't want to work your shift patterns
- Don't want to wear your uniform

Offering the position

Your new team member's voyage should start as soon as you offer them a job with you.

- Consider doing the following:
- Send a congratulations card signed by all the current team members
- Plan their first day to celebrate them. Get out the red carpet, balloons and cakes!
- Prepare them for success

I'll talk more about your team members' voyage later.

Bootcamp

Your bootcamp is the training that is given 'backstage' before the team member starts to officially do their job. Providing this training means that new team members are more confident and have an understanding of the tasks they are going to carry out. It ensures you don't take people on, put them out front and say, 'Get on with it.'

After bootcamp, I recommend that every team member has a learning log that tracks what they've learned and what they still have to learn in their current role before they progress. For example, I would suggest a junior, intermediate, senior and managing learning log. It's important that team members know how they're doing and this is a great way of tracking it.

The ATOAR recruitment process may sound complicated at first. However, if you use the acronym and break down each step, it will save you hours in wasted time and wrong hires, and you'll be able to refine your recruitment recipe and outsource it to one of your leaders. Believe me, it works!

What if you spot brown cow behaviour in your team?

We ask this question at our Blue Cow team events and the answer we hear the most is, 'Sack them!' While that makes everyone laugh, of course, it's not the right answer. First, decide what is brown cow behaviour in your team and ensure everyone knows. Then, if you or any other team member sees it, do the following:

- Tell the person they are being 'brown'
- Ask if they need any help
- If they have a complaint, remind them to go and see the person who can do something about it, not just moan and bitch
- Remind them that being in this 'field' is a choice; if they don't like it, they should leave and go find one they love

Always get legal advice before you let any employed team member go, and never allow bullying in your team.

What happens if you need to move someone on with love?

We always want to act fairly, however we must also act assertively and quickly.

The 'trim your bush' scenario

Imagine you want to grow a beautiful rose bush. You plant the 'rose bush seeds' in your garden, you water them, place them where they will get sunshine, nurture them, maybe even talk to them to help them grow into the beautiful bush. As the seasons change, the roses on the bush may start to wilt. You notice and rather than 'dead heading' (chopping the flower off), you try to help it thrive again by giving more water, maybe some plant food and watch to see how it responds. If it responds well, it may revive however it is does not, you will need to remove the wilting rose, because if you do not, it may well cause a virus to spread throughout the bush.

It is exactly the same with your business. You have planted the seeds for your dream business and team, you have worked hard to grow it, nurture it and you want it to thrive. Team members are like the roses on the rose bush. They have seasons. The seasons vary in length and duration, but they do exist. You may find a blue cow team member starts to 'wilt', if they do, treat them just the same as you would the real rose bush, talk to them, nurture them and wait to see how they respond. If they do not respond positively, act fast. Get legal advice and move them on, 'trim your bush'. Before there is time for a 'brown cow virus' to spread in your team.

Velcro customers

You deserve your business to be full of your ideal clients and customers. Decide who your ideal customers are and focus on attracting and serving them. You don't want everyone as a customer, you want Velcro ones: clients or customers who are going to take your advice, buy your products and services, and pay on time. If you allow non-Velcro customers into your business, they are often the ones who don't get the best results and don't want to pay! Every customer has the ability to become a nightmare or a Velcro, raving fan.

Ask yourself:

- Who is your ideal customer?
- Where do they hang out?
- How can you reach them?

Saying no to non-Velcro customers

You don't have to work with non-Velcro customers. But, unfortunately, you may find yourself working with people who are less than ideal and the number one reason this happens is money. In my experience, non-Velcro customers end up causing more stress and take more energy – as you have to sort out more issues. Added to this, they are often the ones who refuse to pay, or want to pay less.

Be confident in yourself that it's okay to turn away non-Velcro customers. This will leave room for the Velcro ones and, as long as you have a plan to attract Velcro customers (which we'll discuss in the next chapter), you don't have to put up with non-Velcro ones anymore!

Womanpreneur

'Reset Moment'

- Rate yourself as a Blue Cow captain. What do you do well, and what do you need to improve on?
- Assess your current team. Have you settled? Do you have Blue Cows?
- What are the Blue Cow and brown cow behaviours in your team?
- How will you celebrate your Blue Cow team members?
- Do you need to change your recruitment recipe to attract Blue Cows?

6
VOYAGE

'It is not what we do once in a while that shapes our lives, it's what we do consistently'

ANTHONY ROBBINS

There are three voyages in your business that all form part of the empowered business model. They provide consistency and stability to the owner and the business itself:

- The business owner
- Your customers or clients
- Your team members

1. Business owner voyage

I talked at the start about the first three steps of the R.E.S.E.T formula and how we have to work on ourselves first before focusing on our business. Now let's talk about the practical steps a womanpreneur must take to achieve success on all levels. Creating a strong business owner voyage is an important key to doing that.

Your power team

Listen up, fellow womanpreneurs – we all need a power team if we want to grow and run a six- or seven-figure business *and* have a family/ home/ personal life. The power team are the people who all have a role in taking care of the bits of your life and business that you either don't want to do or are not best at doing; or the things that mean you have less time to do the things that really matter to you.

For many years, I resisted a power team. I thought I should be able to take care of all things – business, kids, husband, parents, pets and house – myself. Organising a power team felt like cheating. Or was it that I was convinced that if I wanted something done, I'd be better off doing it myself so it got done properly? I felt like a failure if I admitted I couldn't do everything. I hated being vulnerable and would always reject offers of help.

I hear this so much from other women in business and can completely relate, as this was me. The reality was that when my business was smaller

– and before my family got bigger – I *could* do it all. However, as my business and family grew in their demands, coming home after a full day's work to do the equivalent of another in the home was exhausting. I found myself getting tired, miserable, resentful and spinning too many plates. I also used to think that it was stressful and busy having younger kids, and that I would have more time and energy when they became old enough to not need as much of me. Then I discovered what life was like with teenage kids! I had no idea. Emotions, parties, friends, lifts, extra money, waiting up for them to call to be collected, the 'heated discussions' as these young people want to grow up and form their own views and test mine. One of my biggest challenges has been 'letting my kids be who they want to be' as they grow up and not continually trying to control who they are becoming. Adapting to life where the kids go to bed later than me, eating all the food in the fridge as soon as I fill it up and a whole host of other 'stresses' after a full days work isn't easy. Many womanpreneurs also have parents or elderly family that they need to support and care for who do not live with them. Taking all this into consideration, why on earth would any sane woman, who is running a business full time, think for a moment that they also have time to do the full-time job of running the home, caring for kids, people or animals without any help?

Cracks had started to form. I knew I wasn't keeping on top of all the things that needed to be done at home and at work. My tipping point came one day when I had a busy day ahead at work and I was trying to get the kids sorted for school. The morning routine was always full of rushing, shouting and cajoling. I was brushing my daughter's hair, with approximately four minutes to go before we had to be in the car, when my son came into the room and asked me where his clean top was for his football session that day.

Normally, I relished it when I had the opportunity to demonstrate I had everything under control and could proudly solve whatever question or challenge I was presented with. Most days, I would happily declare that his kit was hanging, clean and ironed, in the wardrobe.

However, on this day, I had the sudden realisation that the top was most likely still sitting in the washing basket – or even lying next to the washing basket where he'd left it the previous week. I'd been away working and I'd dropped the ball. And I *hate* dropping the ball!

Yet, in all honesty, it was my fault. Before I went away with work, my husband had offered to put on washing and I'd said no, I would sort it. Rather pathetically, I was concerned he would 'do it wrong'. I would then have extra work to do putting it right. Not only was I treating my husband like a child, I was disempowering us both. This was at a time before I knew about the power team and having help at home so the washing was down to me.

Suddenly, I found myself having a major meltdown among all the morning chaos, now with only one minute to go before we needed to be in the car. I ended up slumped on the floor, sobbing. I was exhausted even before leaving the house and the kit issue had pushed me over the 'keeping it together' line. I suddenly realised how stupid I was being. Sometimes, I would even hide the dirty washing basket in my wardrobe until I'd had time to deal with it, tucking away the evidence that I was not on top of it! Why on earth was I behaving like this?

Later that day, I decided on all the things I would stop doing – both around the house and in my business – and set up a plan to outsource them. I created the exercise I now call the 1, 2, 3 exercise and I use it with all my clients.

The 1, 2, 3 exercise

Sit down with a blank sheet of paper.

Make a list of all the jobs that need to be done in your home and your business. I mean *everything*.

Let's think about home:

Food shopping
Cleaning the fridge
Taking the bins out
General cleaning
Washing
Ironing
Putting away the clothes
Cooking
Cleaning the oven
Changing the bed sheets
Feeding the dog
Taking the dog for a walk
Taking the cat to the vet
Posting letters
Loading and unloading dishwasher
Sorting cupboards
Tidying up
Removing clothes that no longer fit kids
Tidying wardrobes
Pairing socks
Clearing out the shed
Making sure the children are fed
School runs
Cutting the lawn
Buying birthday cards and gifts
Cleaning cars
Car maintenance
Labelling uniforms

Admin
Decorating
Replacing toilet rolls
Removing the empty used shower gel bottles that are left in shower

Now in the business:

Marketing
Answering the phone
Checking emails
Ordering stationery
Stock check
Getting new clients
Sales
Finances
Social Media
IT
Recruitment
HR
Production creation
Customer service

Add all the activities you do, or that need to be done by someone, into both lists.

Label each task with a number as follows:

1 – You love to do it

2 – You don't mind doing it

3 – You *hate* this task

If you live with someone else, ensure you get them to do the home task list too. When my husband and I did this exercise, we discovered that I *hate* taking the bins out, so it was a 3 on my list, but he didn't mind and it was a 2 on his. So we were able to allocate this task as his responsibility. It may sound a simple solution, but our job is to do our best to stop doing all the 3s on our list.

How can we achieve this?

Step one: do as I did. See if anyone you live with can take on any of your 3s after doing this exercise.

Step two: outsource. Get someone else to do those 3s. I know that some of you will have a brown cow voice shouting in your head right now, saying, 'I can't afford to do that.' However, there are two things to consider here.

- If you really can't afford to pay, consider doing a task swap. When I was starting out in business, I *hated* ironing (and still do). I offered my ironing lady a chiropractic adjustment session a week in return for her doing all my washing and ironing. I have also exchanged cleaning and housekeeping for business coaching; personal training for seminar tickets; proofreading services for car sharing. What could you do a service exchange for? I don't advocate doing this long term as you need to be careful that the exchange is fair to both parties, so set an agreed timeframe before you start. It can all go horribly wrong if you don't set the rules and trial duration from the start.
- Then consider – if you outsource a task you hate, how much money will you save yourself in the long run, in terms of what you spend compared to what you can make in the same timeframe? I hate all things admin. Hiring my first admin assistant allowed me more time to create products and make sales in my business. That brought me in more money than it cost me to pay her for admin. Even more importantly, it gave me time for the things I *wanted* and *needed* to do. Now most of my business admin now is done by others who are not only more talented than me at this, so they actually do it better, it

also frees up even more of my time for work I prefer and am more skilled at. My team are passionate about being awesome and getting things done quickly and effectively, which saves me lots of time, energy and money in the long run. I used to be the absolute worst control freak with micro-management-itis, if I can achieve this, and let go, anyone can.

What tasks are you going to stop doing from now on? Who can you ensure does them instead of you?

Do the 1, 2, 3 exercise now! And then get everyone in your house to do the same: your significant other and your kids (if you have any and if they're old enough).

Essential power team members

Who do you need in your power team? Here are some of mine:

Housekeeper (please kindly note, a housekeeper doesn't actually cost much more than a cleaner – yet does everything!)

My housekeeper understands that her role is to keep our home running like a well-oiled machine. She comes in every day for around two to three hours. We have a checklist she follows that we designed together, with tasks listed and how often they should be done. I treat the process just the same as I would my business. After all, it's even more important than my business because it involves the people I love the most. My husband and kids (and our dogs!). Every womanpreneur should employ a housekeeper. Stop the guilt if you have any and stop the 'I can manage it all myself' thoughts. Also stop any negative feelings you may have about paying someone to do work in your home especially the old traditional 'womans work' that we would most certainly do if we were full time homemakers. You are empowering your housekeeper as you are giving them employment and the opportunity to work in a team where they are respected and appreciated. This is awesome. So work out how to pay for it and empower someone to run your home. If you get the right person, you won't regret it.

Here is my advert that you're welcome to tweak. I posted it in my local community Facebook group.

PART-TIME HOUSEKEEPER REQUIRED

We need someone who can:

- *Help create calm out of chaos in our busy household*
- *Help us keep things tidy and ordered*
- *Walk our dogs*
- *Help with washing and putting clothes away*
- *Sock pairing*
- *Washing up/emptying dishwasher*
- *Cleaning*
- *Occasional shopping*
- *Occasional cooking*
- *Posting letters/parcels*
- *Liaising with gardeners/current cleaning team where necessary*

We will:

- *Pay when we say we will*
- *Give regular set hours – 5–10 per week (possibly more)*
- *Be grateful for your help*

This position is right for someone who:

- *Is a non-smoker*
- *Is a car driver*
- *Likes kids and dogs*
- *Is dynamic and loves organising*
- *Wants regular hours – you will need to be able to work Monday–Friday for some hours every day*

- *Is honest and reliable*
- *Wants to start asap*

This position is NOT right for someone who:

- *Dislikes cleaning, tidying and creating order*
- *Doesn't like kids and dogs*
- *Likes calling in sick on a sunny day*
- *Has no common sense or positive work ethic*

Hourly rate starting range from £10–12 depending upon number of hours and experience.

Please PM me or email. Thanks.

The first time I posted this advert, I had 12 messages in the first 15 minutes. I then set about interviewing them just as I would in my business, using the group interview process.

I also use a housekeeping company where the owner provides the housekeeping team and sorts it all out so I don't have to. This works well too. So you don't necessarily have to employ the housekeeper yourself, use an agency that provides one.

Cleaner

Okay, so I've tried to persuade you to get a housekeeper. However, if I have failed, a cleaner is a must, unless you absolutely *love* coming home from a busy day at the business, sorting the kids, then starting cleaning. I know some of us out there may enjoy cleaning and, if so, fine. But only focus on tasks that aren't a 3 on your list!

If you have a busy household and more people living in the house than just you and one other, you need a cleaner for more than two hours a week. Be honest with yourself. Do you come home from work and then start doing hours of cleaning, house sorting, cooking and washing? As a womanpreneur, especially if you have kids or animals, there will still be plenty you can get involved in, even with a cleaner helping! I used to actually clean and tidy up before the cleaner arrived, as I didn't want her to see my messy house. WTF! What was wrong with me? Now I pick things up and put them away so that she can clean, but I certainly don't clean before the cleaner. Please ensure you don't either!

Personal or admin assistant

Whether you use the same person for home and work or have two separate people, an awesome admin assistant is a must! They can take care of *so* many of your tasks, including all the 3s on your admin list. I recommend you use a virtual assistant if you don't want to employ someone. Create a job description and list all the tasks you want support/help with. Set a three-month trial and a weekly catch-up time. I normally ask my VA for an email update on a Monday morning, where she lets me know which of the tasks are outstanding and if she needs anything from me. We get clarity on what I'm working on and what she is working on and set some deadlines. We also email most days with updates and pending tasks. A great admin person saves you time and money.

I have spoken to many womanpreneurs who are like my former self: they tell me that all the VAs they use are simply not good enough; they just end up taking back the task and doing it themselves because its quicker, easier and less stressful. Just as I say to them: if that's you, then stop it! Find a better VA; great ones do exist. Find one who fits you and 'gets' you, one you can create a partnership with. You are a dynamic lady so you must have a dynamic assistant alongside you!

You may have to search for a while. I tried a few before I found the awesomely amazing side-kicks (aka assistants) I have now. Having great assistants has helped me hugely. Unlike businesses I have had before when I employed lots of people, I now have purely VAs in my team. I have a part time assistant who runs specific projects as I need her and it works really well. Thank you Amy! You rock! I have an awesome events manager, thanks Sue! You are amazing. I also have a full time assistant who gets stuff done, has all the skills I don't have in terms of organisation and admin, and we both have the same work ethic. Even though she's my VA, it feels like she's a fully committed member of my team, just as much as previous team members I have employed. Thank you Ravit, you are awesome. I then call upon project managers, social media, copy editors and marketing team members as I need them. If you get a great team around you, you do not necessarily need lots of them employed by you to create a multiple 6 figure or 7 figure business.

Childcare support

I have never had a paid nanny as I've been very lucky to be able to rely on awesome family support. However, I have also had the benefit of fabulous school support and amazing after-school clubs. Recently, whilst living in Spain, I was home-schooling the kids for a year, so I had a babysitter who helped me. Knowing your kids are safe and happy goes a long way as a womanpreneur. When my eldest two children were little, I was trapped in my business. I remember having no choice but to drop them at nursery, even if they were unhappy, as I had to dash off to work. Too many times to remember I dropped them off crying and they had to be pulled off me. I hated it so much but I needed to work; I wanted to work. We tried a number of different places until we found one I was happy with – and, more importantly, the kids were happy with.

When I got pregnant with my third, I knew I didn't want to go back to those awful nursery-drop-off days. I needed to change things so I had choice and the freedom to be with my kids and still run my business. Luckily, a new nursery opened at my kids' school and child number three wanted to stay every time I dropped her brothers off. Great schools and nurseries make a massive difference. Big thanks and gratitude to Mrs Mason and her team.

So, what did I have to do to achieve the balance of working in our business and having kids?

- Find great childcare options that I was happy with
- Scrap conventional working hours. One of the benefits of owning your own business should be that you don't have to work the typical 9–5 and can choose your own hours that fit in with you and your life. So I decided I would be Mummy until 9.30am every morning (unless I had to travel to a client or to speak at an event), aiming to be there to get the kids up and off to school 90% of the time. I do the school run most days and it's something I love to do
- Schedule meetings and clients so they all start after 9.30am. I find this gives me the time to achieve what I need to as Mummy, without it feeling like a mad rush. Set your working hours to suit your personal life, too. Even if it means other people don't like it. Your ideal clients and customers are the ones who fit in with you
- Stop my calls and meetings at 3.20pm and become Mummy from then until around 8pm. If I still have work to do or calls to make, I do it all then. I explain to my team that if we have a project or deadline, I will work after 8pm to get my work done, but I don't expect them to do the same. I also set my appointments with customers and admin time at times when I'm not being Mummy
- Put my power team in place as already discussed

The hardest part of changing my working hours was changing

my mindset and limiting beliefs about doing so. When I owned healthcare practices, for years I started seeing my patients at 8am, meaning I was often at work just after 7am. Then we didn't close until around 8pm, and I wanted to be there until then too, to ensure everything was running well. I had patients who were used to my working those hours and I didn't want to move them as I felt bad. However, those were the hours I worked *before* becoming a mummy; *before* the business employed lots of other practitioners and team members; *before* I became a business owner and MD of a chaotic house.

Even once our business was able to run without my *having* to be there all the time, I would still 'hang out' and 'be there' because I didn't want my team to think I was expecting them to work harder than I was. I remember saying to my business coach at the time that I felt bad going on holiday, as my team couldn't take as much holiday as I could. Or I'd feel guilty if I took days off. He reminded me about 'golf course' business deals – that plenty of business is done on the golf course. The team may think the owner is just playing golf again but this isn't true. I realised that when I took time away from the business, I would always come back inspired, refreshed and with new ideas and strategies that the team would benefit from. If I hadn't taken time away, I would have got stuck in the noise of day-to-day issues, from which it isn't a strong place to drive the business forward.

In the end, I just had to 'get over' what other people thought and, generally, no one complained about working when I wasn't there. Each team member was treated respectfully, encouraged, had great working conditions and was paid on time. I invested lots of time in them so they had a good work-life balance, and most loved working in our team.

Please kindly note, even if you don't have kids (so can't blame them

to hit the ground running when you go back to work. Why is this so important? Because, as business owners, we sometimes take less holiday than we would as employees. Be as strict with yourself, as you would someone you love very much, who you want to keep happy, healthy and well. It's not the Blue Cow way to work so hard that you forget to build a life you love. Working constantly will lead to your becoming a brown cow: burned out, friendless and depressed. Be in control of your life.

The 90-day rule

Every 90 days, take 3 days away from your business. It gives you space to reflect and see the business differently. Time away is hugely important for business owners, who often find themselves sorting out issues and getting stuck and tired. Literally, get a wall planner, mark out the blocks of 90 days and ensure you take three days off after each one. It doesn't mean you have to go away on holiday, it just ensures you get a break. As one of my mentors, Brendon Burchard, says: as entrepreneurs, we are working on our business – creating, coming up with ideas, discussing next steps *constantly*. The 90-day rule is a way of allowing us some recharge time.

Declutter

I don't know about you, but in our busy household we are great at accumulating 'stuff'. I have an awful habit of piling paperwork and post into a carrier bag and putting it aside to sort 'later'. Later never seems to come, of course, and, before long, my office is full of lots of carrier bags packed with things to be sorted. My other habit is that I don't like to throw away things I may want to use later. I always take those little bottles of shampoo and shower gel from hotel rooms and, if I'm really honest, I even take the shower cap (well, I have paid for it) and I never even use a flaming shower cap! My bathroom cupboard was full of them for years! When I used to hire a seminar room, I had to bring home all the unused paper and pens, flipchart paper and water, just because I'd paid for it and might need it in the future. These are great for the kids to use. Now I have so many of these items stashed in my cupboards, I tell the delegates to take them instead.

I also used to have lots of things that I kept for 'later,' which turned into years because 'later' never seemed to arrive. I kept clothes that didn't fit me including a black pair of size 8 PVA trousers I would wear out dancing at university when I was 20. I mean why does a 44-year-old, currently size 12 mother of 4 kids need those in her wardrobe? (Please can I note there is nothing wrong with PVA trousers, this is not my issue at all, it's the fact that they were 20 years old and there was no way I was ever going to fit in them without a serious plan that is not on my current agenda). Eventually, I went through and chucked out all the clothes that no longer fitted me but that I had been keeping for when I *could* fit into them again. Not only did I feel good having the clear out, but it felt good giving them to charity.

When my husband and I decided to move to Spain for a year, we had planned to rent out our home in the UK. So, I decided to be ruthless. I created a system:

- Going in the skip
- Going to charity shop
- Going into storage

I went through every room in our house – every cupboard, drawer, wardrobe – and I cleared everything. It was hard at first as I found myself with lots in the storage pile. Then I decided to change tack slightly. I found it easier to give things away if I thought about giving them to a women's refuge. I imagined that, instead of my stored items sitting waiting for me, they could actually help a woman who had had to leave her house suddenly with nothing. Using this method, I was able to be a lot more giving.

I love to journal. I have journalled for years and, as a result, I had tons of used-up notebooks. I sat one afternoon and read through many of them, some of which were from a particularly stressful period of my life. I cried, laughed and felt all sorts of emotions. I started to put them all in the storage pile and then my husband asked me why I was keeping them. I had never even considered getting rid of them until that moment. It was a very emotional decision but I spent a few hours reading and ripping them up, and then had a little ceremony where I put them into the skip. I knew I had done the right thing because one particular journal was written whilst I was expecting our eldest son. I sobbed buckets when I read my messages to him when he was growing in my belly; my thoughts about his premature arrival six weeks early; the landmarks he had reached as a baby. My son actually came in whilst I was looking at it. I explained I was keeping it for him. He read a few pages and said awkwardly, 'That's really nice, Mum, but I won't need it.' At the same time I asked him if he would want the hundreds of paintings I had kept since he could first hold a paintbrush, a mix of very artistic 'masterpieces' (yes, I am biased), hand prints, leaves etc. He laughed and gave me a big hug. 'You're all right, Mum,' he said. 'Chuck them and the journal!' At first I was gutted, I couldn't throw them out. However what was I keeping them for? My kids were not interested. So, into the skip it all went. However, I did decide to keep a keepsake box for all of them, which included things like their hospital bands and first outfits.

After having a good clear out and declutter, a lovely thing happened. I felt lighter. Some of those journals contained painful memories of difficult times in my life, so it felt like I was moving on and putting those times behind me. As a result, I continued ruthlessly until the house (and shed) was completely culled. IT FELT AMAZING! I know some of you will be horrified that I got rid of those things; however, clearing out the past creates room for your future. I suggest to my clients that they do the same thing and many reply that they don't have the time. I completely get it. However, I strongly recommend you find the time somewhere or employ a decluttering manager. Contact one of my friends who specialise in this area. Sara Stevens (from the Home PA service) or Nicola Lewis (from 'This Girl can organise') can definitely help you via our free Blue Cow Women in business FB group. It is a *very* liberating process.

Money mindset, financial abundance and wealth

Your business should serve you, both emotionally and financially. We all have the ability to create wealth and financial abundance. However, that doesn't mean we all will. Your business should make money, give you a great income and allow you to increase your net worth. If your business is *not* earning money then, let's face it, you should call it your hobby and get a job.

Your relationship with money will be very important when it comes to the success of your business and yourself as a womanpreneur. We all have a 'money blueprint' that affects how we see money. This blueprint will have been influenced by our childhood, our parents, school and other friends, and the part of society we grew up in or live in now. Are you a Blue Cow or a brown cow when it comes to your 'money language'? What are some phrases that you associate with money?

Look at these:

- Money doesn't grow on trees
- Do you think I'm made of money?
- Money is the root of all evil
- Money makes the world go around
- You don't need money to be happy

Or what about:

- I deserve to have lots of money
- I deserve to be a millionaire
- I'm entitled to be rich

Womanpreneur, you deserve to have lots of money and be financially abundant! Unfortunately we may have a money blue print from childhood that challenges this belief. We may have inherited negative beliefs about women earning money or earning more money than a male partner or perhaps more than our parents earned. It has not been that many years since women were not allowed their own bank account, mortgage, and couldn't have some jobs unless they were married. Analysing your money blueprint and developing it into one where you are ok with financial abundance and wealth is very important. If you feel dis-empowered in this area, please start the process of brainwashing yourself and getting some financial education to change your mindset.

Your being financially abundant is very important. If you only have enough money just for yourself to survive, you cannot help others. You deserve lots of money, regardless of how much you grew up with or what your parents earned, or the salaries of your friends and relations. Your struggling for money does not have to be your future! Becoming financially abundant requires you to create a business that earns money and ensures money flows to you.

Know your break-even for your business and life

Many womanpreneurs (and men) tell me they don't like talking about money. You need to get over this if you are in business. Money is just an energy that is exchanged for a great product or service. Don't shy away from it!

Your break-even is: to have no profit or loss at the end of a business activity (Cambridge dictionary meaning). How much money does your business have to bring in each month to cover its costs? It is amazing how many business owners (especially women) do not include a wage in their breakeven. They would never take a job that declares they will not be paid (unless they knew it was a volunteering position) yet they run a business but not factor in paying themselves. This is not good.

In terms of what you pay yourself, how much do you, personally, need to cover all your expenses each month for your personal life? Your business needs to make at least this much or you will end up in debt. Of course, we all want our businesses to earn much more than this so we can make a profit, have money to reinvest into the business, and also pay ourselves well. To work out your break-even, first, go to your bank account and add up all the standing orders and direct debits that go out every month. Then look at your business and add up mortgage or rent, wages and expenses. Come up with a total and set your break-even so you can work out if your business is on track to cover it. Those of you who are already smashing the break-even, well done! Now you should set some financial goals as you grow your business. Monthly targets that you can track are important so you can tweak your strategy as your business grows.

Check your pricing

So many womanpreneurs have their pricing set in a way that doesn't serve them.

'*Would you buy this cake?*' I saw this question posted in a business forum recently.

The post had lots of replies from well-meaning womanpreneurs who'd all answered with a resounding 'yes – it's an awesome cake.'

However, in my reply I asked, 'How much is it? The price would determine if I would buy it. It is a lovely cake, though.'

The lady responded, 'How much would you pay for it?'

Woah, that is a huge question!

So let's talk about pricing in your business (and the price of the cake). The two questions the lady asked above do not take into account three important factors:

- The lady's avatar or target client
- The method, vehicle and place for selling the cake
- What I (the customer) want the cake for?

Imagine the cake is one of many of the same cakes sitting on the shelf in a supermarket such as Asda. It is priced at £5. There are many there just waiting to be bought. Would you buy this cake? If you were looking for a cake for an everyday-type occasion or family gathering and if you had £5 in your budget for it, you may well purchase it.

Now imagine it is your child's birthday party. The theme is 'Hello Kitty' as your daughter loves everything Hello Kitty. The local bakery has a Hello Kitty cake. It's priced at £12.99. Would you buy the cake? What would you think about the price?

Next, imagine the cake is being presented at a wedding show. The cake is a one-off, bespoke design and you can adapt it to make it more personal to you so it becomes one of a kind. The cake price is listed as £80. It can be delivered to your venue and comes with a lovely cake setting. Would you buy the cake? Perhaps you would if you were getting married. What would you pay for it? If you really wanted the cake and you'd allocated that budget, maybe you'd be happy with the cost of £80.

Now imagine we have a vase. The vase is glass, medium sized and has a delicate pattern around the rim. You like the vase. At

Selfridges in London, the vase is priced at £80; at Tesco, it's priced at £20; at the local car boot sale, the vase costs £2. It's the same vase. However, our decision as to whether to buy it or not will be dependent upon how much we want it. For example, if we saw it at the boot sale we would make a different buying decision than the one we'd make had we spotted it in Selfridges. At the boot sale, we may well buy it 'just in case we need it'. But I doubt we would think this way at Selfridges.

Whether or not we buy it would also be decided by the purpose for which we are buying it. For example, is it for our grandparents' special wedding anniversary? If so, we might go for Selfridges and get it gift-wrapped beautifully, rather than choosing to buy at the boot sale, because it's for their special event. Now don't get me wrong, I love going to boot sales and have got myself lots of bargains over the years. However, what I pay for items there is very different to what I would expect to pay (even for the same item) in a high-end store. Why is this when it's the same item?

When deciding the price point for your product or service, it's important that you look at whom the product or service is aimed, who your ideal client is, how you are going to deliver the product or service, and how you are going to package it. Are you packaging it like the high-end store, Tescos, or the boot sale? Once that decision is made, ensure you go into the right marketplace to sell it. If you are selling it where your ideal client doesn't exist, or in the wrong place, then you may well hear frequently that your products or services are over- or under-priced, and you won't sell as many of them as you could if you'd made sure these two things were in alignment.

People make buying decisions based on emotion, and there are two types of purchases.

1. **The 'distress' purchase.** We make these purchases to solve an immediate problem. For example, if someone has severe back pain, they head to the chiropractor to get a quick resolution. Or, someone might have a broken boiler, so they call the boiler expert out because they want to get the problem solved urgently.
2. **The 'want' purchase.** This is a purchase we may not *need* – but we *want*. Let's consider a couple of these: maybe a designer handbag or a Rolex watch. If you need a bag, you can get something non-designer and cheaper. And if you want to be able to tell the time, you can achieve this without having to buy a Rolex.

So where does your business fit? Are you selling a product or service as a 'distress' or a 'want' purchase? Or do you sell a mix? And what are your current prices? When was the last time you increased them? How are you packaging your product or service? Is it high end, middle tier or cheaper? This will impact how much you sell.

So many of the clients I work with are under-charging. In fact, many have their pricing completely wrong. I frequently help them redesign and put their prices up, once we have reviewed the product or service and target market to ensure they are aligned.

Don't reduce your prices thinking you will make more sales! First, check you are promoting your business to the right audience and customer. A great mantra is, 'My price is a reflection of my skill, not your budget'. This is something useful for us to remember. Your clients are paying you for an outcome, not your time – so price accordingly. This is an important consideration for the womanpreneur and her business owner voyage.

Your business cash flow

I was recently running an event and a lovely delegate told me that one of the biggest challenges in her business was cash flow. This is a really common challenge for many of the womanpreneurs who come to me. As already mentioned, if your business is not making money, it's a hobby! Probably an expensive hobby that actually costs you money.

So let's look at how to increase cash flow in your business:

- Decide on the product or service you are selling
- Decide on the price point
- Decide on your ideal client
- Look at where your ideal client 'hangs out'
- Set the targets and methods to reach your ideal clients
- Design the voyage from first contact to last
- Introduce a product grid that encourages your customers to buy multiple products from you

Product grid

I have a client who owns an ironing and dry-cleaning business. When we first started working together, her business offered one service: dry cleaning. As we developed her product grid, we brainstormed all the other items that could be offered to the customers currently using her services and which of these would fit with the business intention. Here are some we came up with:

- General washing of clothes
- General drying of clothes
- General ironing
- Holiday offers – get a suitcase drop.

The idea is that you design a product grid for your business where your ideal customers can purchase more than one product or service.

Consider what other products or services you could be offering that you aren't currently.

Pots

One of the challenges with cash flow is that clients start by telling me that although the business makes money, after paying the bills and other outgoings there is little or no money to pay themselves. Thus begins a cycle where money comes in and money goes out, and everyone else gets paid – except for the business owner.

I generally suggest that the business owner sets up pots. Pots are sub-accounts that come off your main business and personal bank accounts.

Examples of business pots may include:

- Current account from where bills are paid
- Tax account where you put the money to pay your tax bill
- Savings account

You set up standing orders for amounts to be transferred from your current account into the other accounts on the first of the month. The minimum is £1. However, as your business grows, you can increase the amounts that you put into the pots.

Personal pots may include:

- Current account
- Tax account
- Holiday account
- School or nursery fees
- Savings

Again, when you pay yourself, ensure that you put money into these pots *before* you spend your monthly money. What sometimes happens is we pay our bills and living expenses and end up with no money left to put into our savings. The key is to put money in the pots first – automatically, via standing order – so you don't notice it has gone from your current account into your pots.

Net worth

It's also a good idea to calculate your current net worth. Your net worth is a personal balance sheet. You can calculate it by working out the difference between your liabilities and your assets. In other words, what you own minus what you owe. Our goal to increase net worth is to increase our assets and decrease our liabilities.

Robert Kiyosaki, author of the awesome *Rich Dad* series, defines assets as 'anything that puts money into your pocket'. Whilst a liability is 'anything that takes money out of your pocket'.

For many people, their home is a liability, as it takes money out of their pocket to live there. Even if you have paid off your mortgage, you still have insurance, upkeep and maintenance. However, if you have a house that you rent out and the rent covers the mortgage and expenses, the house is an asset. But if that very same house becomes empty or someone damages it and you have to spend money on it, it then becomes a liability. So, whether the house is an asset or liability depends upon cashflow. If cashflow comes in, it's an asset; if cashflow is going out, it's a liability.

Examples of assets:

- Cash
- Your home is an asset but a mortgage on your home is a liability. This suggests that because a mortgage is a debt, you need to pay it off before your home is really considered an asset
- Stocks

How to convert a liability into an asset

According to Kiyosaki, financial education involves six basic words:

- Income
- Expense
- Asset
- Liability
- Cash
- Flow

The secret to being financially abundant is 'can you control cash flow?' Financial intelligence is the ability to do this.

Please read the *Rich Dad* series! This will really help you with learning more about wealth creation.

The womanpreneur business owner voyage is hugely important. We must ensure that our business is serving us on all levels (including financially) and allowing us to live a life we love. If it's not doing this currently, it's time to change it!

Womanpreneur

'Reset Moment'

- How is your money mindset?
- Are you charging what you should be?
- Are you paying yourself what you should be?

2. Your customer voyage

Your customer voyage begins from the moment that customer makes contact with you. It is the steps that are taken to allow the customer to move from an enquiry to being a customer. The voyage should be consistent and to the same standard throughout, so the same amazing experience is created regardless of which team member your customer interacts with.

But when and how does this happen?

The four voyage phases

Your business is like a bucket with holes in it. This means that every month you add new customers into your business. You want them to stay and become repeat customers, as opposed to leaving without even buying your product or service – which would mean you'd have to go and find more new clients. The stronger your customer voyage is, the less need there is to find new customers, as the bucket does not empty out every month. It keeps partially full with current clients. And it costs your business less to keep customers than it does to constantly be marketing for new ones because you're not taking care of the ones you already have.

As a womanpreneur, you must know how your customers arrive and what is their voyage in your business. You should know who the top buyers are and recognise them. The 80/20 rule says that 80% of your business will come from 20% of your customers. So knowing your KPIs (key performance indicators) when it comes to the voyage, and where each customer is on that voyage, is important.

The voyage can be thought of as a funnel. The funnel is wide at the top and narrows at the bottom. There are four voyage phases (VPs) in a client's voyage, and I refer to them as VP1, VP2, VP3 and VP4.

Voyage phase 1 (VP1)

VP1 occurs at the point the customer makes contact with your business. They may approach you in person or by phone after being recommended by a friend, or they may check out your website after seeing one of your promotions, listening to a podcast, reading your blog or seeing your social media output. That first contact is all about VP1.

VP1 is the start of the relationship. It has to answer three main thoughts a potential new customer has in their mind at that early stage:

- Can this person or business help me purchase what I am looking for?
- Will this product/service take me to where I want to get or solve my current problem or need?
- How does this person/these people/this business make me *feel*?

Remember, people are buying an outcome, *not* just your product. You need to demonstrate that you can solve their problem or need before you start trying sell to them.

Voyage phase 2 (VP2)

VP2 is all about the formal process of facilitating a 'sale' and turning a *potential* new customer into an *actual* customer.

The transition from VP1 to VP2 should be a smooth and easy procedure with as few moving parts as possible. VP2 is often considered a 'lead conversion phase' by many businesses and, as such, it can cause stress for business owners and their teams because of the inherent risk of appearing 'salesy' and inauthentic. However, if the time the customer has spent with you at VP1 is compelling, and the three questions that are most pressing are answered, the act of buying from you is a logical progression from one thing to the next.

Voyage phase 3 (VP3)

VP3 is the step-by-step process by which the product or service is delivered in a world-class, consistent way, ensuring that the desired outcome is gained. You achieve this through a set of systems specifically designed for your business and ideal customer.

Systems systems systems

For many years, my husband and I talked about systems in our business. I became obsessed with the awesome work of Michael Gerber, creator of *The E Myth Revisited*, and I wrote hundreds of systems for our business, many of which are now used by our consulting clients in their businesses.

However, during our coaching with Michael, we discussed the difference between having systems in your business and systems with a Blue Cow culture and team. There is a massive difference between a 'staff' member who delivers a system and a Blue Cow team member who is delivering a WOW experience using the system in line with your culture and Blue Cow ethos.

After my husband and I had been talking systems with our team, one awesome Blue Cow asked us why we called our processes 'systems'? She said she felt we offered much more than 'systems' and should change the name to 'recipes' as this was much more fitting for our Blue Cow business. After this, the term 'recipe' was born and everyone talked about 'recipes' as opposed to 'systems'.

The recipes became the step-by-step voyage that made up *how* we consistently delivered a Blue Cow customer experience. Every team member was coached in each recipe. Each person opted into ensuring the recipes were never diluted and remained consistent for every customer, regardless of who was taking care of that customer.

Team stress levels went down and customer satisfaction went up due to the team knowing how to carry out every task in our business with consistency and the same intention.

The recipe book

A world-class customer experience doesn't just happen. Create a *front stage* and a *backstage* recipe book.

- Front stage: all the recipes that are used to create a Blue Cow customer service experience – what the customer sees and experiences
- Backstage: all the recipes that are required to run the business, including recruitment, holidays, contracts, handbooks, training plans, stocktake, finance. The customer does not see these. They run so smoothly; it appears as if they don't exist.

The recipe book – just like a cookbook – lists everything needed to create your business and enable it to run like a well-oiled machine.

Imagine that you want to bake a beautiful chocolate fudge cake. You are excellent at making these. However, you ask your friend to make the cake while you do another task. But instead of having a step-by-step recipe and list of ingredients, she 'makes it up'. Just as you are about to tuck into the creation, your friend realises they have forgotten to add the chocolate to the mix. So you have a cake, and it may actually taste okay, but it certainly won't be the gorgeous chocolate fudge experience you were expecting! Ultimately, you're disappointed.

Your business is exactly the same, it needs recipes, ones that will achieve a consistent, client-centred outcome every time.

Think of your business as a West End theatre show. It has a cast. Each cast member has a role to ensure the show is a success. If one of the cast is absent, someone else can step in and the show is equally successful. Much of my husband's and my stress in the early days of business ownership was because we did not treat our business in this way. We didn't have a recipe book or understudies to ensure the show went on if someone was away. It would seem crazy for the actor playing Romeo to go on holiday, leaving the show to go ahead with Juliet on her own. But this was what was happening in our business. It was being affected by holidays, sickness and absence in our team, which in turn affected our capacity to see patients and decreased the income. We didn't have rules – and that meant we were fire-fighting most of the time; reactive rather than proactive.

If a member of the team left suddenly or called in sick, or something else went wrong, it put a huge strain on the rest of the team because there was no strategy in place to deal with it. So, thinking of the business as a West End show took a lot of the emotion out of it, and we made sure that the team knew that 'the show must go on'. Whether they were a practitioner or a receptionist, they had a responsibility to find someone to replace them in their absence. That way, the show would always run the same as normal. Once this was implemented, we weren't worried about individuals being indispensable. Don't get me wrong; we loved every single member of our 'cast'. However, the show did not rely on them individually. Our business success was not affected by what was happening in the lives of our team members, either front or backstage.

Here are some examples of front stage recipes that a service-based business would certainly require:

- How to answer the telephone
- How to deal with new customer enquiries
- How to greet a new customer

- How to make an appointment (if applicable)
- How to open up the centre or shop
- How to take payment and how much to charge
- How to process a customer on the computer
- How to give a receipt
- How to cash up
- How to make a sale

Backstage recipes might include:

- Company handbook
- Job descriptions
- Contracts
- Recruitment checklist
- Appraisal forms
- Holiday forms
- Pay forms
- Stocktake
- HR folder for each team member

You name it, there must be a recipe for it! The goal is to ensure that every team member plays their role as a positive, happy advocate for the business. Each new team member should be coached in the recipes, which are there to ensure that not only can your business run with less stress, but the team is also able to deliver outstanding client service. Recruit well so that people who love to take care of others, who are Velcro to your business and in alignment naturally with your intention, will use your recipes.

With this in mind, also watch out for the mediocre staff member who will happily tell you, 'I don't need recipes. I know how to answer the phone or serve a customer.' What they are saying is, 'Leave me to answer the phone *my* way, thank you. I don't need you interfering and holding me accountable for not doing it the way you want it done.' It is staff members like these who build empires in your business and prevent you from taking it to a world-class level. So watch out!

Creating your recipes

As mentioned, the purpose of your recipes is to achieve the intention of your business – consistently. They are step-by-step guides that you and your team use to ensure your clients get a consistently great experience. This is never more important than at the voyage step of this process.

Unfortunately, many business owners tell me they haven't got time to write recipes, as they are too busy running the business or 'putting out fires'. However, although time-consuming at first, once written, learned and acted upon, your recipes will take your business and your life to new heights. If you have multiple businesses, it is almost guaranteed that the one where you spend the most time is the most successful and profitable. So work on creating a strong client voyage.

Heads up – look out for indications of a weak voyage:

- Poor customer service – lots of complaints about silly mistakes
- Inconsistency of service
- Team members 'making it up' and getting things wrong
- Perceived indifferent attitude from the owner, manager or team member
- High turnover of new customers
- Poor customer retention and lack of repeat business (of course, it depends what business you have but most businesses want a customer to repeat purchase or spread the word to other potential customers)
- No referrals

World-class businesses do not leave the customer voyage to chance.

Please kindly note, when your business is smaller, you may undervalue the importance of recipes, thinking you're doing all right because *you* ensure that your team gives a great customer experience. However, as your business grows and you have more customers, running it without recipes will bring stress, and ultimately lead to dropping the ball – which may mean a decrease in your customer experience and outcome, and an increase in your (and your team's) stress levels.

The best time to work on your recipes is before you need them! Plan for growth!

Voyage phase 4 (VP4)

This part of the customer voyage will be discussed in a later section, as it is the 'visceral' component of the Blue Cow 5 V Technology.

3. Team member voyage

Just as your customers will go on a voyage in your business, so will your team members.

They need to be able to progress in their roles, and I suggest having junior, intermediate, senior and managing levels. Each level has a written role expectation, pay scales and learning log so the person can be measured and assessed, making a clear path to progress to the next level.

This certainty and clarity will bring stability to your team members, to your business and to you. Don't ignore the need for this.

In addition to having formal development levels, you should create an emotional voyage, as each individual will have a unique set of emotional needs. We are not referring to a tears-and-tantrums type of emotion but to something more profound. Blue Cows will feel passionate about your business and that means they will feel emotional towards it. It will matter to them.

Each team member has deep wants, hopes and dreams that they hope will be achieved there. Each will be unique. The job of the business owner or manager is to find out what these are. The best way to do this is to get to know your team members. Take them for coffee and ask them: 'What's important to you? Where do you want to go? What do you want to achieve?' Create a space for them to be honest with you. Some of their wants and desires will be business related, some will be personal.

Start as you mean to go on

The team member voyage begins when they first make contact with you, *not* on their first day, once they have already started. As we discussed in the Velcro section, the Velcro and voyage start from the first advert, the emails inviting them to the group session, the observation, the bootcamp and the job offer. You want every new team member to feel amazing that they have managed to secure a place in your team. If you want your team to WOW your customers, treat them like Blue Cows from the start.

This is an example of a team member voyage (once you've used the recruitment recipes I outlined in the Velcro chapter, offered them a job, and they have accepted):

- Give them a written offer and a contract (sounds obvious but you'd be surprised how many businesses don't do this)
- Send a congratulations card signed by yourself and the team – giving social proof (social proof means the new recruit gets positive feedback from others already on the team)
- Give them a WOW first day – literally put out a red carpet.

Introduce them to other team members. Have cakes at lunchtime

- Give them a Blue Cow buddy who helps them settle in. This is especially important if people have relocated to work in your team. They may need somewhere to live, and someone to show them where the local supermarket or gym is
- Give them a coaching timetable for the first two weeks so they can learn the job role. Set times they need to be at coaching before they are 'left to it'. You don't want new team members finding themselves feeling abandoned.

Never just give someone the job and let them get on with it. Blue Cows won't stay.

When they begin, team members are what we call 'unconsciously incompetent'. This means they don't know what they're going to need to know. Once they've been working with you for a while and have had some coaching and training, they'll move to a 'consciously incompetent' stage. This means they now realise *all* the things they are going to need to know. They may start to compare themselves to experienced team members and start to feel *doubt*. At this point, some great people will leave if they are not supported and reassured. The next stage is 'consciously competent'. This is where the team member starts to feel confident and can carry out their role. The final stage is 'unconsciously competent'. They do the role, following recipes, without having to think about it.

Managers and senior team members are often in the final stage. They should be cognisant of these levels when they are working with new team members, otherwise your business may lose great Blue Cows at the 'consciously incompetent' stage, when they are having doubts.

Some things to remember when leading a Blue Cow team member's voyage:

- It is said that you have to tell someone something 27 times before they 'get it'. Don't get frustrated if your new team members takes a little while to grasp what you are teaching them. Factor this into their voyage
- Every Blue Cow team member will need reassurance, support and coaching during their voyage
- Avoid micro-managing your team. This does not lead to a compelling team member voyage

In a seminar with business owners, after the discussion about creating a compelling team member voyage, one of my clients joked, 'So are you saying I need to pay them *and* praise them?' Although this comment was greeted by lots of laughter from the other business owners in the room, the answer is clearly YES! All humans, especially Blue Cows, need recognition, appreciation and approval to thrive – and definitely pay them too!

Important points to note:

Blue Cow approach

- Ensure you create a compelling voyage for yourself, your Velcro team members, and your customers
- Your customers deserve great customer care experience every time they visit
- Recipes set the business owner free to work on the business and give their team clarity and an opportunity to shine whilst delivering a consistently WOW experience
- Don't leave the customer's business and customer experience to chance or personalities. Create recipes and a compelling voyage.

The brown cow approach

- Without recipes, your business will be inconsistent
- No team member voyage – you cannot create your dream team if you don't see them and communicate with them!

- If you're 'chained to your business', you'll end up burned out, fed up and struggling with money.

Womanpreneur

'Reset moment'

- Describe your customer voyage – list the steps from the first contact to end
- Assess your current voyage for your customers
- Do you have a recipe book for backstage and front stage? Is it used by your team?
- Review your team member voyage – how well are you at looking after your Blue Cow team members and letting-go-with-love non-Velcro ones?
- Is your business serving you?

7
VISIBILITY

'Be so good they can't ignore you.'

STEVE MARTIN

All over the world, there are womanpreneurs who have great products and services but businesses that are not making enough sales. Without customers, the owner becomes frustrated, disillusioned, worried and starts acting like a brown cow. The business is ultimately going to fail.

Visibility is the thing most business owners are obsessed with from the very beginning: they want to know how to get more new customers. While it's imperative your business becomes visible, it should only be the focus once the preceding three Vs are in place. Most business owners get that the wrong way round: they want to become visible before the vibe, Velcro and voyage are fully set up. This leads to a whole host of challenges, especially when customer experience is less than it could or should be, and this ultimately damages the reputation of the business.

For example, imagine a healthcare clinic that places adverts for more new patients. The new patients arrive – however, there is a poor vibe, poor velcro and a weak voyage. The patients don't get a great experience so they leave, the owner puts out the next advert, and the process begins again. Or imagine a cleaning business where new clients have a first session but the cleaning team do a poor job as someone is off sick so they're short staffed. Those customers are unlikely to return. That said, once the first three Vs *are* in place, visibility is, of course, vital.

Getting your business visible

Getting your business visible and securing new customers should not be left to chance. It's a military operation that needs a strong set of recipes for success. The great news is that, once you have put the visibility systems in place, they become cyclic, meaning you don't have to keep reinventing the wheel.

I suggest you get a wall planner to record your visibility promotions so you can see in advance what you have coming up. Set a target for how many new clients or customers you want to attract (lead attraction) and convert into paying customers each week (lead conversion). Then you can set the visibility plan to meet this target. If you track it each week, you will know if you are on target and if your strategies are working. If you're not hitting new customer targets, you can tweak your visibility plan. Attracting your ideal number of new customers does not have to be a challenging task if it's done with intention and consistency.

Your ideal customer

When it comes to filling your business with clients and customers, one thing business owners often forget to consider is who their ideal clients actually are. Often owners are so desperate to build their businesses, they feel they never have the luxury to narrow their market; to niche it down. Three years into the healthcare business I owned with my husband, I came to the decision that I wanted to see children and babies. I'm passionate about kids and chiropractic. We changed the channels by which I was attracting new patients and, very soon, I attracted more of those I desired. Within 12 months, my client list had completely changed. I had never been so happy in business! This would not have been possible if we hadn't been focused on becoming visible in this new niche.

In my mentoring business, I have a clear definition of who my ideal client is. There is one key criterion – especially important if I'm working with them one-to-one – which is that they will be action-takers. They will be people who are going to invest in themselves and take the required action to make the changes they desire, in line with the goals we set, so they get results. Therefore, I don't take everyone who may enquire about working with me. I've discovered over the years that my non-ideal (non-Velcro) clients who don't take as much action complain more, and give off negative energy. Also, they don't like to pay their bills on time or spend as much money investing in themselves as my ideal clients.

You should consider who your ideal customers are and then set the strategy to attract them.

There's a member of our Blue Cow Women in Business Facebook community, let's call her Victoria, who makes the most beautiful bespoke gifts for children. They may include name banners, which not only look amazing but the buying experience is exceptional, too. Victoria allows the client to choose the colours used, the font, the design and decoration, and is happy to add jewels, unicorns, bows, flowers – whatever the customer wants to make the design more personal. Her customer voyage is amazing. However, her visibility plan was all wrong.

Victoria's is a high-end product. If someone wants a cheap, mass-produced name sign for their child's bedroom, they can buy it elsewhere. Victoria's ideal clients are those who want to invest in a beautiful gift for their kids or someone else's. They most likely have the cash to spend on such items and prefer the handmade quality and unique buying experience (voyage) that Victoria offers. But where should Victoria advertise to become visible to these ideal clients? Victoria became frustrated as she was selling her beautiful work at local craft shows, where she was told her items were too expensive. I talked to her about getting visible, and the need to reach her ideal customers through high-end boutiques, referrals, and distribution channels that sell similar bespoke products.

It wasn't that the items were too expensive (trust me, they're more than worth the investment), it was that Victoria was getting visible in the wrong way to non-ideal clients. This made her doubt herself and her product. If she could rethink her visibility plan, target the ideal customers, and change the method by which she was becoming visible to them, her business could really take off. And I hope it does, as she deserves it.

Types of visibility

Visibility is the central pillar of marketing your business.

In a Blue Cow business, the best strategy for generating new customers has two visibility facets:

- Internal promotions
- External promotions

Any business will feed off of a combination of both of these.

First, let's consider what the differences are between external and internal visibility strategies.

External strategies

- Community awareness
- Talks
- Social media
- Website

Internal strategies

- Referrals
- Customer promotions
- Customer appreciation parties if service-based businesses.

External visibility

Community awareness is where you go into the community where your ideal customer 'hangs out' and connect with them personally. Let's imagine that you're a healthcare practitioner looking to attract patients who are in pain and want your help. You could organise a talk to a group that may include your ideal clients, for example:

- Sports clubs
- Mother and baby groups
- Golf clubs
- Tennis clubs
- Gardening groups
- Art clubs
- Women's groups
- Church groups

If you own a dry-cleaning company and your ideal customers are professional people, you may choose to join a club where they go, or, if looking for business owners, maybe you would join a business networking group. In order to get suggestions, ask your current ideal customers where they 'hang out'. Ask them to introduce you to the organisers of the different groups and say you offer free talks to their members. At the end of the talk, give them a compelling offer for your product or service.

Designing your talk

Your talk should comprise a start, middle and close.

- The start should include some kind of opt-in to engage the group. If you're a specialist in back pain, you may ask the group, 'Does anyone here suffer from back pain?' People who do will put a hand up. If you run a cleaning company, you may frame your talk to be about 'how to avoid black mould in your bathroom' (or a useful cleaning tip)
- Introduce yourself and explain why you are passionate about talking to the public (even if you are *very* scared to start with!)
- Tell them what you want them to know about your business and

what you offer (keep it simple and a maximum of 30 minutes. You don't want it turning into a hostage crisis situation!)

- The middle of your talk should be content led
- At the end of your talk, you should give them your compelling offer – *if* they take action today. For example, as a cleaning business, you could offer a free home-cleaning consultation

Social media

There are plenty of social media gurus who will be able to give you awesome social media strategies better than I can. However, I've learnt whilst growing my businesses and helping hundreds of other business owners to grow theirs that you do have to have a consistent social media strategy. Importantly, not just generic posts. You want to have posts that show a mix of social proof and credibility.

The strategy should be consistent, where you post regularly, and posts should contain:

- A mix of pictures for social proof – showing your happy customers with their products or receiving your services, not just a photo of the product
- Testimonials from happy customers, singing your praises and telling the world how awesome your product or service is
- Credibility pieces – this means you show yourself at work, either with a client or making your product
- Offers (but not too often)
- Calls-to-arms to contact you
- Positive life quotes that will appeal to your ideal customers
- Pictures of you in 'normal life' or your team in action – customers love to see the real you!
- Valuable free information that makes them want to check you out

What you don't want is a load of generic social media posts that do none of the above. It's a very personal decision how much of your outside-business life you show. I tend to avoid posting photos of my kids. However, I appreciate that, in a service-based business with a guru model, people do like to feel they can get to know you, and this is only achieved if you show them snippets of your personal life as well as business.

I show lots of business photos with clients: at events, when I'm travelling, writing, or creating products, and maybe recording or interviewing someone. I plan my social media posts so that I know something is going into my free groups and onto my pages every day to keep it consistent. I normally do this first thing in the morning so they're not missed. I do know lots of business owners who outsource their social media, which is fine as long as the posts achieve what you want in terms of attracting your ideal customers.

When planning to use social media, one key factor in getting visible is to be *findable*. One of my awesome mentors, Myron Golden, says, 'A customer who finds you is worth much more than a customer you find.' Find Facebook groups where your ideal clients hang out, serve in the group, give free advice and support. Deliver outstanding value for free, so people think, 'WOAH, if this is the free stuff, what is their paid-for service or product like?' Don't make the mistake of thinking I am saying go into someone else's Facebook group and sell your wares. This doesn't work. People like to buy from people they like – so be likeable and authentic, build relationships and don't just try to sell to them.

Your website, SEO and becoming 'Google-able'

When you search on Google for someone important, someone visible or someone who is 'doing stuff' in the world, usually a bunch of things will come up: articles, photos, videos, their website and their social media pages. That's because these types of people exploit the 'must-use' sites to make them web-famous. Google loves these sites and rates the information on them very highly:

- YouTube
- Instagram
- Pinterest
- Facebook
- LinkedIn
- Twitter
- WordPress
- Snapchat

It's important to remember, however, that your success both on- and off-line will only be as good as your intention for your business. If your message isn't strong, then you will be left behind.

Please be sure that you do not spend lots of money on external marketing if your customer voyage is weak. It is just a waste of time and money. You will attract the new client only to lose them very quickly. I have worked with many many womanpreneurs who were trapped in this cycle for years leaving them frustrated, attracting the wrong customers and spending too much money for little return.

Internal Visibility

Your referral strategy

Referrals should not be left to chance. Most of your customers will not think to refer someone to you unless you or one of your team specifically asks them to. Your job is to enthuse your customers so that they become raving fans and tell everyone they meet about you and your business. Enthusiastic customers will make referrals – dissatisfied or unhappy ones won't.

Remember, we are talking about a feeling. Help your customers get great results or the outcome they want from your product or service and make them feel amazing. Then they'll tell everyone they know!

If a new customer arrives as a referral from one of your current customers, we suggest you do the following:

- Acknowledge the referrer to the new customer
- Send a handwritten thank-you card to the person who made the referral
- Send the referrer a discount voucher for a different service or product within your business (usually a 'want' purchase!)
- Put a Blue Cow referral celebration board out each month, either in the 'bricks and mortar' business or on the website or Facebook, saying, 'HUGE thanks to the following people for referring their friends and family to us during the month of ...' Then list their first names only and the first names of the people they've referred. This is a great social proof tool and so easy to track

I recently did a business consultation call with a womanpreneur who runs a business selling kids' pamper parties. The owner reported that she wanted to get more business, and found giving out flyers generally wasn't working. I suggested some tweaks to her plan, which included:

- Getting a testimonial from each client after a party and including this in her visibility plan
- Getting lots of photos of happy-looking customers for social proof (always get signed permission if you are going to use these pictures in your marketing, especially if children are involved)
- Giving each customer a referral gift voucher for them to pass on to their friends (as well as everyone who attended the party). She was already giving a business card but the problem with that was there was no social proof and no call to action to actually refer
- A repeat business plan – recording the dates of all the parties, especially if they were birthdays, and sending an 'Are you

ready for another pamper party?' a few months before the next birthday or event. You can do this with siblings too as the child who had the party last time may have moved onto new party ideas
- Growing her community and creating raving fans who would refer more people like them

I teach my clients when and how to ask for referrals and I also explain the 80/20 principle that states that 80% of our business comes from 20% of our customers. I have seen this so many times, not only in my own businesses but in my clients' businesses too. Not everyone will refer – so, treasure the ones who do!

Client storybook, or 'What our clients say about us' booklet

Another excellent internal visibility promotion tool is the customer storybook. Some of my business owner clients show me a rather dull 'testimonial book', which is just full of lots of writing! The less writing the better.

The customer storybook I recommend you create is similar to this but much more compelling. It's a combination of customer 'stories', pictures and thank-you cards. This is the chance for your customers to tell the narrative of their experience in your business. They don't have to gush or 'big up', or sell you and your products or services to anyone. They just need to tell the truth: how they felt, what happened to them, and how the product or service helped/transformed/delighted them.

New customers should be given access to the customer storybooks at specific points along the client voyage so they don't miss out on seeing them. There will be photos, jokes, stories and titbits in them that encourage your connection with the client and vice versa.

Storybooks are great for social proof and credibility and are a chance for you to show off without showing off. Think about the UK magazine, *OK*. It's filled with photos and not too much writing. Create your storybook in much the same way.

Customer appreciation parties

If you run a service-based local business, consider holding a party once a year and inviting your ideal customers. It may sound a bit odd. However, building your community in this way is a fabulous visibility tool. Not only do you invite your current ideal customers, you encourage them to bring their friends, meaning you get to celebrate with them *and* give a special offer at the event to those people they've brought with them. You don't have to spend huge amounts of money. I've done low-cost events like a cheese-and-wine party right up to a high-end charity ball. The aim is to show your customers you appreciate them, build your community and combine this with a visibility strategy.

Get your team involved

Visibility should not just be left to the business owner. Involve your Blue Cow team members. Here are some ways to do this:

- Make visibility part of the team culture
- Give your team referral vouchers so they can actively encourage referrals
- Encourage your team to celebrate referrers
- Set rewards and bonuses when your team helps organise visibility talks and events
- Rota your team to attend visibility events

Once you've created your visibility plan, *measure, measure, measure!* Keep a record every month of which promotions brought in the new customers. Also, note what the ROI (return on investment) was.

Know how much the promotion cost to run and the number of new customers that came from it. If your business doesn't have as many new customers as you'd like, don't despair! It's probably not to do with your product or service. You're just not getting visible to the right audience. If you feel your product or service is correctly priced for your target market, rethink your visibility plan to ensure you're reaching it.

Points to note:

- High visibility is a combination of internal and external strategies that should not be left to chance
- Surround yourself with team members who are motivated to spread the word and get involved
- Have a wall planner with your internal and external promotions listed for the year ahead
- Set targets for the number of new customers each month and ensure you meet them with your visibility plan
- Review – is the strategy working? Tweak it if you're not reaching your targets
- Build your community so it's full of raving fans who refer customers just like them

Beware:

- No visibility plan and complaining about not having enough new customers
- No targets set for numbers of new customers
- No review of the strategy to ensure it's working
- No team involvement – visibility left to the business owner
- Not taking any action, feeling defeated and frustrated
- Starting to doubt your product or services when it's your visibility strategy (or lack of it) that's the problem

Womanpreneur

'Reset Moment'

- Imagine your ideal customers. Describe them (young, old, sporty, financially challenged or solvent)
- What is your monthly target for new customers?
- Buy a wall planner and start to fill it up
- Assess your current internal and external visibility strategies
- List other strategies you will now start using

8
VISCERAL

'All lasting business is built on friendship'

ALFRED A. MONTAPER

'Visceral' is the penultimate step in this Blue Cow 5 V process. The dictionary defines 'visceral' as 'characterised by or proceeding from instinct rather than intellect: a visceral reaction'. If you intend your customers to continue to use your products and services for the long term, the visceral component is something you should ensure is in place.

Being visceral means appealing to emotion rather than logic – it's as simple as that. It means your customers *love* to stay as part of your business community and use your products and services repeatedly. The relationship becomes ongoing.

I am a terrible nail-picker and biter. As a result, I like to have my nails regularly manicured in the hope that they'll look lovely when I work with my clients or speak at events (as well as them looking nice for myself). I've had my nails done at a variety of places but I'm a loyal customer to one of them. So why do I keep going back? Yes, they do my nails really well and I'm pleased with how they look. This is obviously a given or I would go elsewhere. However, the visceral component is how they take care of me, as if I am 'one of them', every single time I visit. I get priority appointments; everyone knows my name; they always go the extra mile with me, meaning I get my special drink; they know me and, no matter whom I see, they joke about the fact that I always look at the colour chart, then invariably go back to one of two colours I have been having for years. Their business has a 'visceral' effect on me.

Many of my clients say they worry about getting new customers in their business. However, if they focused on looking after the ones they have and getting the visceral component correct, they wouldn't need as many new customers because their business would be full of those who love to keep buying from them.

But how can you and your business be more visceral?

First, implement the first 4 Vs. The degree to which you implement these four will be the degree of viscerality you build up between your business and your customers. Once you've done this, offer a formal mechanism by which your fans can become visceral: a membership, a subscription, a buy-in – something that makes them part of a community or a tribe. Most importantly, create a visceral product that requires an ongoing bank-to-bank transfer of funds to 'stay in', for example, a direct debit or standing order.

Every service-based business can do this and most online businesses, too. I have set up memberships and visceral communities in healthcare, gardening, cleaning, dry cleaning, ironing, beauty, administrative services, gift sales and make-up.

Benefits to the business of being visceral and having a membership or subscription service

- A community full of raving fans/members who love what your business does
- Clients and customers who are happy to pay regularly
- Membership fees coming into the business every month via standing order or direct debit

Plus, it's great fun serving business advocates.

The customer's voyage should automatically transition to the visceral component and it should be a seamless process.

Points to note:

- Build a membership or subscription service within your business that your clients and customers want to stay part of
- The membership community will actively refer more people like themselves

- The community will give amazing social proof to newer customers

Avoid:

- Hard selling, contracts or fear tactics do not create a great membership community
- Membership isn't about sign-ups. It's about creating a passionate, vibrant community
- Losing clients to other businesses because you don't have a *visceral* component in yours.

Womanpreneur

'Reset Moment'

- What are your thoughts on creating a membership or subscription service?
- What steps will you take to create and grow it?

9

T: TAKE ACTION (AND GROW SOME BIG HAIRY BALLS)

So there you have it, this is the R.E.S.E.T. formula. These are the steps you need to create a six- or seven-figure business *and* create a life you love. The most important part of the process is what you *do* with the knowledge you now have. Will you take action? Will you be willing to transform from where you are right now to where you want to be? The 5 V technology can be scaled as much as you like, depending upon what business you want.

Your final task is to DREAM BIG and then TAKE ACTION to put all these things together and make them work for you.

MINDSET + STRATEGY + ACTION = TRANSFORMATION

This morning I did a call with a lovely womanpreneur who was very emotional and felt very stuck. At the start of our call, she reported being fearful about money, her work premises, her landlord and her ability to provide for her family (she is the main bread winner). Her mindset was dis-empowering her and she could not see a positive way to move ahead. We talked though some options that would move her forward and she agreed to decide and then take action. We set a two week deadline. The path is much clearer for this awesome lady, however if she chooses not to take action, nothing will change for the better. Things will ultimately change because as time passes the situation will get worse. I find this a lot, womanpreneurs who may have got lost, just as I was all those years ago, fearful to take action and giving their power away. Inside each one of us is a Blue Cow who wants to get unleashed. A warrior womanpreneur who is strong, yet willing to be vulnerable, who refuses to settle and believes she is enough to achieve her dreams. Trust me, she is in there. If you are lost, please don't despair, I urge you to use the RESET formula. It really can turn your business and your life around, if you are willing to let go of where you are right now. Sometimes we have to let go of the good, to allow in the great.

In terms of taking action, here are some daily considerations for all womanpreneurs:

1. Create your daily 3 MUSTS. These are the three top things that will push your business forward
2. Live in gratitude. It is hard to be frustrated and unhappy if you focus every day on what you are grateful for
3. Trust that where you are right now is where you are supposed to be
4. Avoid feeling overwhelmed. We all get days like these. Use your inner Blue Cow guidance system to know, on days like these, you need to take a day off
5. Regularly review the process, as it is easy for dilution to occur, so you don't go off track
6. A small, consistent amount of action is much better than one huge bit of action and then nothing for ages
7. Avoid procrastination
8. Ask yourself, 'Is what I am doing right now taking me towards my dreams?'
9. Write your ideal day. Review and celebrate it as you start to experience it. The more you implement, the more of these you will have. Life can be full of ideal days if you decide it
10. Celebrate your wins, no matter how small. Don't move onto future goals without doing so

The message I want to leave you with is something I recently posted in the Blue Cow Women in Business FB community **www.facebook.com/groups/bluecowwomeninbusiness/**:

REMINDER: whether we like it or not, sometimes as a woman in business we must grow some 'big hairy balls' ... to achieve the success, happiness and freedom we deserve on our terms. Our business MUST serve us and we must not allow ourselves to feel disempowered by focusing on fears, doubts or anxieties … not feeling enough or worrying about being 'rejected' by team (staff) or clients who prefer things to be their way, leaving everyone happy except you has to stop. There is an art to leading well enough so everyone feels like they win. Ultimately, you are in control of who represents you in your business and your own happiness. You are awesome. You have got this. Flap those 'BIG leaders' hairy balls' about … and feel proud of the AMAZING strong Blue Cow womanpreneur that you are!!! You are not alone … we are walking right beside you.

So go forth, do not be scared. You CAN do this. Grow those balls, unleash your inner Blue Cow and do what you need to do: take action to empower yourself and create a business and life you love!

YOU DESERVE IT.

CONNECT WITH ME!

Join our free Women in Business Facebook community
www.facebook.com/groups/bluecowwomeninbusiness/

If you'd like to explore how we can work together please email my team: **team@bluecow.online**

Check out my websites:

If you are a womanpreneur
www.jodavison.com

If you are a health care practice owner:
www.bluecowpractice.com

WHAT JO'S CLIENTS SAY ABOUT HER

Working with Jo has simply changed our lives. With her support, guidance and encouragement we've moved our business to new levels and have strategies in place to continue to push forward to achieve greater goals and our ultimate dreams.

I am forever grateful for finding Jo and all that she has help us do so far.

Caroline Carter

Jo is nothing short of amazing, she and her team have revolutionised our business, and we will be forever grateful! Thank you.

Laura Pendleton

This lady is on fire she's such an inspiration! Her drive, determination, positivity is out of this world.

Kate Everett

Working with Jo has really changed my life. It's given me the confidence to pursue creating the business of MY dreams! If you're considering doing it, please don't put it off just go for it!

Felicity Crone

Jo is an inspiring business woman, she is amazing and I recommend every business woman to join her community . A more supportive group you won't find anywhere else!!

Ravit von Springer

I would like to take his opportunity to thank Jo for her continued motivation, her bountiful energy and her masterful way with words, which make her stories and advice so much more effective.

Sharing the same space as Jo and being in her presence has made me realise what I truly wanted from my life and how I was going to make this dream my reality.

Komal Vadi

Jo you are the most amazing lady I have met in my life. You are the best mentor one could ever have wished for and your skills and knowledge are priceless. I have learnt so much from you Jo and each time I meet or speak with you, I learn more.

Thank you

All of you out there have to join Jo to get your entrepreneurial dreams to be realised.

Bharti Ladva

Working with Jo has been amazing. She has managed to help me through both personal and professional challenges over the last few years. I continue to be monitored and coached by Jo. I can now say, hand on my heart, I enjoy running a business, I enjoy my team I work with, and have strategies to overcome most, if not all, obstacles that my work life throws at me! Thank you Jo x

Rebecca Ashby

Jo Davison and her community is a must for anyone who is looking to surround themselves with positive, creative, thought leaders and disrupters. It's a place to bounce ideas, share honest emotions and be expertly inspired by Jo to make every day a Blue Cow day.

Lucy Cassidy

Knowing Jo and being part of my journey she expanded my horizon beautifully ... everything and anything is possible - limitless opportunities - feeling gratitude X

Jasminka Hansson

Jo Davison has been inspirational in changing my life so that we are not chained to the business ... if you are a women in business this is the place to be... you can not afford NOT to be part of her community...

Mandeep Marway

I am totally blown away by what an inspiring speaker Jo is! I've come away with so many ideas and more importantly been given so much guidance. Thank you Jo - I can really see the way you have inspired Felicity who is a wonderful boss and mentor for me, and we're only just at the beginning of the journey!

Vanessa Louise

Working with Jo helps you focus and prioritise to reach your goals. Jo strikes the balance of sharing her wealth of experience and ideas plus giving you a metaphorical "slap" when you need it. (Those that know her will find this funny!). Throughout the process, Jo is supportive and motivating at just the right times. Thank you for the "slaps" just when I needed them. X

Julia Pullin

Life changing, practice changing, life liberating process. It's comprehensive, challenging, thoroughly worth it and I would recommend it unquestionably.

Julien Barker

I have had great support from Jo as I balance being a business owner/entrepreneur, wife, mother and all other roles I have to be. I feel empowered to create the dream life I want for me and my family and not have the guilt that so many women go through balancing business and family life.

Angel Koonar Turner

Jo has opened our eyes to our dreams, so that they can become reality. I cannot thank her enough. It's hard work but so totally worth it. Living life to its fullest = freedom to me. Thankyou Jo.xx

Laura Green

Working with Jo is a mix of many things:

- *having the opportunity to ask questions and learn from someone who's been there, done that more than once, plus got more than one T-shirt to prove it.*
- *the chance to network with, and support likeminded people.*
- *the knowledge that we are not isolated or alone as business owners (and it's all too easy to think that we are)*

Jane McKenzie-Riley

Having the opportunity to work with Jo on specific business and personal projects has been amazing. We get much more done and are held accountable to make sure it happens. However, if the process uncovers other areas along the way that require attention, Jo calls on her experience, knowledge and network to make sure that we address everything.

Spencer Pullin

Jo has been such a great mentor. I needed some clarity and guidance through the launch of my online platform. I had looked in various places, looked to other mentors for help, but they just didn't match up either to my expectations or their promises. Now in Jo I found she understood exactly what I needed, how to guide and direct me to achieve the goals we had set. It's all done with lots of laughter and a great GSD attitude!

Without Jo's help and support I wouldn't be as far down this road, and I definitely wouldn't have enjoyed the journey as much! Thank you.

Emma Fretwell

BIG LOVE AND THANK YOU

To my core power team:

Ravit: for helping me create the space I needed to complete this book project. Thank you for nagging me when required and still loving me when I was driving you mad. You are totally awesome and I am blessed to have you by my side. **Amy:** for all your encouragement and amazing skill proofreading this book, giving suggestions and ensuring editors' ideas were added. **Wanda:** for being an awesomely inspiring editor. Your passion for making this project a success, your advice and suggestions kept me going in the moments when I was feeling doubt. **Alexa:** for your great copy-editing and helping me push the project forward. **Andy:** for being fabulous at designing this book. You have delivered exactly what I wanted. **Amanda:** for fantastic photos. Making me look much more photogenic than I actually am. **Sue:** for being my brilliant events manager. You take care of the details so fabulously that I don't need to worry. **Jermaine:** for being an amazing speaker, MC and source of inspiration. **Andrew:** for being my world class AV team. Your ability to stay calm whilst ensuring an event runs smoothly is second to none.

Stephanie and Leah: for helping me transform from tired, over worked mummy, into a 'glamorous' speaker. **Fiona:** for organising all our travel brilliantly. Sorry for any grey hairs I have caused. **Sara:** for all your support, home PA work and the awesome massages. **Kerry and her fabulous housekeeping team:** for your wonderful organising of our home. **Laura:** for always going the extra mile for us and for loving Tilly as much as we do. **Julie:** for keeping our clothes 'wrinkle free' and giving me more writing time. **Mrs Mason and her team:** knowing AR is happy at school, especially if I've needed her to stay later.

To my Blue Cow Universe Family:

We have created a unique, amazing community that I am proud and grateful to be part of. Thank you to those who have invested in our mentoring, taken action (or are in the process of taking action) and transformed their businesses and their lives. It brings me joy to be on this voyage with you. Big thanks for being so giving and supportive in our BCU. Everyone who has referred their friends, sent their team members on our courses, given us amazing testimonials and are a constant source of happiness in my world. For me it is much more than a business relationship. Though there are too many of you to thank personally here, I want you to know that I'm grateful to every single one of you. I love 'being in the trenches' with you. You have given me plenty of fodder to include in this book.

To great mentors (I have had many, so am focusing on the ones at the time of writing):

Anthony Robbins: So many pivotal business and life moments have come from your inspiration and strategy. **Russell Brunson:** The time you spent talking with our son Louis meant so much, he became my seminar buddy and we have shared some special times together that we might not have experienced otherwise. **Les Brown:** You and I ran 'together' every day during the time I was writing this book (until I got pregnant and then, to be honest, we walked). I laughed, cried and took lots of action to get this book done after your words of wisdom. **Shaa Wasmund:** One of the things I love about an awesome mentor and friend is their ability to see things from a different perspective. The 'suggestion' you gave us seemed simple, however it was a total life game changer. Not only did it influence where our family lived whilst I was writing most of this book, but it will positively impact our family legacy for our kids. **Daniel Priestley:** I have learnt lots from you as a mentor and friend that has helped me in my quest to serve the people who can benefit from my message. Thank you for going the extra mile for me and demonstrating that there are 'good people' in this industry. **Sara Blakely:** Although we have not met personally (yet). Thank you for your inspiration and for being an awesomely, inspiring Blue Cow Womanpreneur. (.... and for everything you have done for my 'butt' and 'baby belly'... they are very grateful ;))

To my family:

My two amazing mums, Ann and Margaret; Huge thank you for everything you do for me and our family. I am very grateful to have you both in my corner. **My dad, John;** I remember sitting in your office chair as a little girl pretending to be running a business. I am sure I get a lot of my entrepreneurial spirit and drive from you for which I am very grateful; **my forever friend, Micky; my precious 'babies'; Harry, Louis, Alice-Rose, and Emilia.**

And Steve. You saved my soul. This book would not exist without you, but more than that, I would not be the person I am without you. Thank you from the bottom of my heart. 143 x